THE LITURGICAL BOOKS

IS VOLUME

109

OF THE

Twentieth Century Encyclopedia of Catholicism

UNDER SECTION

X

THE WORSHIP OF THE CHURCH

IT IS ALSO THE

96TH

VOLUME IN ORDER OF PUBLICATION

Edited by HENRI DANIEL-ROPS of the Académie Française

THE LITURGICAL BOOKS

By LANCELOT C. SHEPPARD

HAWTHORN BOOKS · PUBLISHERS · *New York*

BX
1970
S47

First Edition, October, 1962

NIHIL OBSTAT

Joannes M. T. Barton, S.T.D., L.S.S.

    Censor Deputatus

IMPRIMATUR

Georgius L. Craven

    Vicarius Generalis, Epus Sebastopolis

Westmonasterii, die XXVIII AUGUSTI MCMLXII

H-9524

CONTENTS

INTRODUCTION

At the present time the Roman rite is used by the great majority of Catholics throughout the world. It is contained in the official liturgical books and these form the principal source of liturgical law. Liturgy is the prayer of the Church and for the Church to recognize it as her own it must be in conformity with the laws that she has laid down: " 'The sacred liturgy is the entire public worship of the mystical body of Jesus Christ, namely of its head and members.' Accordingly 'liturgical' are those sacred actions which, from the institution of Jesus Christ or the Church and in their name, are carried out in accordance with the liturgical books approved by the Holy See, by persons legitimately deputed. . . ."[1] Organization of the liturgy of the Church is the function of her hierarchy, for the liturgy is the prayer and praise of God's people and their coming together for worship is presided over by the bishop (as successor of the apostles) or by his delegate, ordained by him for this purpose. If in the past decisions on liturgical matters seem to have been taken by civil authorities—Charlemagne, for example, imposing the Roman rite and liturgical unification on his empire—it is clear that such things were done with the consent of the hierarchy. Since the Council of Trent, which effected liturgical uniformity in the West, it appertains solely to the Apostolic See to organize the liturgy or approve liturgical

---

[1] Instruction of the S. Congregation of Rites, *De sacra musica et sacra liturgia* (September 3rd, 1958) translated by J. B. O'Connell. The quotation with which the extract begins is from the Encyclical *Mediator Dei et hominum* (November 20th, 1947), hereafter referred to as *Mediator*.

books (canon 1257). Before the Council of Trent, as will emerge in the present short history of the liturgical books, considerable latitude was enjoyed by local bishops both in compiling liturgical books and in ordering divine worship throughout the territory under their charge.

Nowadays the official text of a liturgical book is contained in what is known as a typical edition (*editio typica*), one, that is, which is printed under the supervision of the S. Congregation of Rites and promulgated by it. All other editions must be in conformity with this typical edition and when a publisher produces an edition of a liturgical book it must be submitted to the local bishop for him to certify that it is an accurate reproduction of the official edition (*Concordat cum originali*). Editions of liturgical books are sometimes issued by the S. Congregation of Rites incorporating small modifications; in this case, without being made new typical editions, they are published as *juxta typicam* (in accordance with the typical edition) or *prima, secunda,* etc., *editio post typicam* (first, second, etc., edition after the typical edition).

THE LITURGICAL BOOKS OF THE MODERN ROMAN RITE

First in importance is the Missal: *Missale Romanum ex decreto sacrosancti Concilii Tridentini restitutum.* This, like the Breviary, was issued during the pontificate of St Pius V (Bull, *Quo primum tempore,* July 9th, 1570). The last typical edition was that issued under Benedict XV (July 25th, 1920) but the reforms mentioned below in connection with the Breviary necessarily entailed a reform of the Missal as well so that the decrees of 1955 and 1960 apply both to Missal and Breviary. In addition the reform of the Holy Week liturgy (decree of November 30th, 1955) affected the contents of subsequent editions of the Missal.

Next comes the Breviary. It contains the choir Office for

every day of the year and is usually published in two volumes, sometimes in one (known as a *totum*); in the past it was often divided into four volumes, one for each season of the year. The full title is *Breviarium Romanum ex decreto sacrosancti Concilii Tridentini restitutum.* It was first published by St Pius V (Bull, *Quod a nobis,* July 9th, 1568). Reforms were effected by St Pius X (Bull, *Divino afflatu,* November 1st, 1911), Pius XII (decree, March 23rd, 1955) and John XXIII (*motu proprio,* July 25th, 1960). An extract from the Breviary containing all the Hours of the Office except Matins, containing, that is, the Day Hours, is called *Horae Diurnae*; it is used on account of its convenient size, but its history and evolution is naturally the same as that of the Breviary.

With the Breviary must be associated the Martyrology (*Martyrologium Romanum*) since it is used at the public celebration of the Office. Its definitive edition was issued by order of Gregory XIII (Constitution *Emendato jam,* January 14th, 1584); the latest typical edition is that published under St Pius X in 1914. The current edition is that of 1956 (*quarta post typicam*) which, save for the addition of notices relating to subsequently canonized saints, reproduces the edition *prima post typicam* (approved by the S. Congregation of Rites, January 11th, 1922). This was the edition severely criticized —very rightly—by historians.

In the third place must be considered the Pontifical, the book used by bishops in those functions specially reserved to them: *Pontificale Romanum* published by order of Clement VIII (Brief, *Ex quo in Ecclesia,* February 10th, 1596). Leo XIII (August 3rd, 1888) effected important changes as did Pius XII; the latest reform (part II of the Pontifical) is that of 1961 under John XXIII. With the Pontifical must be considered the *Ceremoniale Episcoporum* first published by Clement VIII (Brief, *Cum novissime,* July 14th, 1600) which gives directions for episcopal ceremonies and functions in cathedral and collegiate churches.

The Ritual (*Rituale Romanum*) is to some extent derived

from the Pontifical. It provides the rites for the administration of the sacraments by a priest and for certain other occasional offices such as the blessings of persons and things, rogation processions, funerals and so on. Its first edition was published by Paul V (Brief, *Apostolicae sedi*, June 17th, 1614). The most recent editions are those of Pius XII, *editio typica* (1952) and *editio prima post typicam* (1953).

The above are the principal liturgical books of the Roman rite. The others, which are extracts from those already mentioned or else contain the plainchant settings of the various rites and offices of the Church, need hardly concern us here. For the sake of completeness a list of these books is given in an appendix to this volume with a few remarks about each.

When St Pius V issued the reformed Missal and Breviary certain dioceses and religious Orders were able to keep their old liturgical usages, either a complete rite, like that of Milan or of the Carthusians, and in this case the Roman liturgical books are not used at all, or merely certain features pertaining to one or other books of the liturgy, as at Lyons, for example, where an adaptation of the Roman Missal is in use but the Breviary is the Roman Breviary with a local supplement.[2] Some places have retained merely a local Ritual (this is the case in Spain as it was until recently in England) or in late years have been authorized to use a bilingual Ritual.

PLAN OF THIS BOOK

In the successive chapters of this book the history and development of each of the principal liturgical books is treated in order. Necessarily to a large extent the history of a liturgical book is the history of the rites that it contains and for this reason it will be found that the Breviary has been given more extended treatment than the Missal: the Mass

---

[2] Further details will be found in *The Mass in the West* in this series.

and its history have already been covered in two volumes in this series[3] while so far there has been little or nothing about the Breviary. It must also be borne in mind that though it is convenient thus to treat the history of liturgy in the West by considering the evolution of the liturgical books in turn such a view needs to be corrected by an overall consideration of liturgical history, for, despite the neat compartments into which we tend to divide it, Christian worship is a unity

[3] *History of the Mass* by F. Amiot and *The Mass in the West* by Lancelot C. Sheppard.

CHAPTER I

THE ROMAN MISSAL

The Roman Missal contains the formulary for Mass according to the Roman rite for every day in the year. A history of the Missal therefore is a history of the rite of Mass from the beginning until the present day. The existence of a book containing the rite of Mass implies, however, a certain fixity of formularies and we know that in the Roman rite this stage was not reached until some period between the fourth and sixth centuries. Previous to this, although the general arrangement of the rite and the content of various prayer formulas followed a traditional pattern, much was left to the celebrant, who improvised round a central theme inherent in the nature of the rite and deriving both from the accounts of it in the New Testament and the nature of our Lord's command, "Do *this*, in memory of me". All this forms what may be called the pre-history of the liturgical book we now know as the Missal.[1] Its history proper begins with what are known as the Sacramentaries.

THE SACRAMENTARIES

The history of the Sacramentaries is somewhat involved. The word itself, which has an obvious connection with *sacrament* taken in its widest sense, denotes a book for the use

[1] See, in this series, F. Amiot, *op. cit.*, pp. 11–17. Detailed treatment will be found in J. A. Jungmann, *The Mass of the Roman Rite (Missarum Solemnia)*, volume I, pp. 7–32, 44–9; *The Early Liturgy*, pp. 10–109. See Select Bibliography at the end of this book.

of the celebrant at all kinds of sacred functions, containing the priestly formulas for the whole liturgical year and for other circumstances. Its evolution takes us back into the prehistory mentioned above.

Quite early in the history of Christian worship the need seems to have arisen to write down at least the typical formulas, and the existence of Hippolytus' tract *The Apostolic Tradition* is some proof of this. Indeed, the fact of improvisation by the bishop in his church does not necessarily imply that in all circumstances, everywhere, all celebrants were able to officiate without some form of *aide-mémoire*; once forms are written down they tend to become fixed and it is not surprising to find in the Sacramentaries themselves traces of these early written formularies. Little books (*libelli*) appear to have been used on the occasion of the Roman stations and for domestic celebrations of the Eucharist. These *libelli* were the immediate forerunners of the Sacramentaries.

Some idea of the complexity of the history of these Sacramentaries can be obtained from an examination and description of the principal manuscript sources. There are three principal types of Sacramentary—the Leonine, Gelasian and Gregorian, the two latter containing some subdivisions. In this description of the Sacramentaries the use of the names which would seem to ascribe them to Leo, Gelasius and Gregory must not be taken as any more than a convenient convention. St Leo, it seems fairly certain, was not responsible for the Leonine Sacramentary; his name has been used in connection with it since its first publication in the eighteenth century and it has thus become a means of identification which it would be inconvenient to drop.

The Leonine Sacramentary

In about 1730 a manuscript was discovered in the Verona chapter library (Codex LXXXV) and was published five years later by Joseph Bianchini in the fourth volume of his lives of the Roman pontiffs. This is the only manuscript known of the Leonine Sacramentary and belongs to the seventh century. It cannot therefore be ascribed to St Leo the Great (pope 440–61) but there is general agreement that the latest portions of the contents date probably from *c.* 540 so that the Verona manuscript is a copy made about a century later.

The Leonine Sacramentary is certainly of Roman origin, though from internal evidence it appears that it was never an official liturgical book in the same sense as the Gelasian and Gregorian Sacramentaries. The fact of its Roman origin can be proved from the topographical references that it contains: it always mentions the Roman Empire with peculiar loyalty and "it exhibits on every page those topographical touches which enable us to distinguish between a text drawn up for the Church of Rome locally, and one which is merely in conformity with the Roman use".[2]

The private character of the book seems no less certain. "It is a private compilation", says Mgr Duchesne, "in which various materials of different age and authorship have been gathered together without much attempt at order."[3] The disorder in which the book has been compiled gives the impression that it formed a collection of models gathered haphazardly from various Roman sources, possibly for the most part from a primitive Roman Sacramentary. The beginning of the manuscript is missing and thus we are without the ordinary and canon of the Mass. The various Masses are grouped according to the months and begin at the end of April, but chronological order is not very carefully followed so that often the Mass of a vigil follows that of the feast which it should precede. In the same way the December Ember Days follow Christmas. In all this disorder there are two points of importance to notice in connection with

[2] *Christian Worship: Its Origin and Evolution* by L. Duchesne, translated from the third French edition by M. L. McClure (London, 1903), p. 139.
[3] *Ibid.*, p. 140.

the history of the Missal. Firstly, in the manuscript there may be discerned a certain number of *libelli* forming self-contained units which seem to show the transition between the period of *aides-mémoires* mentioned above and the time (? end of the fourth century) when the bishops were recommended, though not obliged, to use a written formula instead of improvising. *Libelli* were drawn up by certain bishops for their own personal use while others, rather than compose their own prayers, had recourse to those used by the pope, having them copied at the Lateran where a collection was kept of the *libelli* of famous popes.[4]

More important still is the contribution of the Leonine Sacramentary to our present Missal. Of the thousand or so collects that it contains no less than 175 are taken from this source, and there is reason for thinking that some of these collects at least can be attributed to St Leo or to St Gelasius (pope 492–6).[5]

The Gelasian Sacramentary

The most ancient manuscript of the Gelasian Sacramentary is that of the Vatican library (*Reginensis lat. 316*). It is in uncials and dates from *c.* 700, and is probably a copy made in France. Although it is the oldest manuscript known it is not in its primitive state. Some changes seem to have been made in Rome and it was subsequently adapted to the use of the Church in Gaul. The manuscript begins with the words: *Incipit liber sacramentorum Romanae Ecclesiae ordinis anni circuli.* The name Gelasian was only given to it in the seventeenth century and is obviously erroneous. Nevertheless, although the whole book cannot be ascribed to the pope whose name it bears, there are certain vestiges in it of an

[4] Cf. A. G. Martimort (Editor): *L'Église en prière* (Paris, 1961), art. "Sources de la messe romaine" by N. M. Denis-Boulet, p. 282.

[5] The best edition of the Leonine Sacramentary is Dom Mohlberg's: *Sacramentarium Veronense*, Herder, Rome, 1956; probably the most easily available edition for readers in England and the U.S.A. is still C. L. Feltoe's: *Sacramentarium leonianum*, Cambridge Univ. Press, 1896.

archaic liturgy some elements of which may well have originated under Gelasius.

The Gelasian Sacramentary differs from the Leonine in that it was an official compilation, though "official" should not be interpreted quite in the way that it is nowadays. In Rome itself there was some diversity of usage. A. Chavasse[6] seems to have established quite definitively that the Gelasian Sacramentary is a Roman Sacramentary, despite the fact of certain elements added in Gaul (for the most part relating to the Pontifical) and that it was written for the use of the priests of the Roman titular churches—namely, that it was a presbyteral Sacramentary and not a papal one and that thus there were two Sacramentaries in use at Rome at the same time—the Gelasian for the use of the priests of the titular churches and the Gregorian for papal use. Finally, and this is a conclusion of some importance, it seems certain from an examination of the text that we can postulate the existence of an older Roman Sacramentary in the proper sense of the word, later than the Leonine but earlier than the Gelasian.

Liturgical uniformity, in the sense that we know it today, certainly did not exist in Rome in the sixth and seventh centuries and in setting out the chronological order of the Sacramentaries it is important to notice that a later recension did not necessarily supersede an earlier one. The various recensions of the Gelasian Sacramentary can be set out as follows:

1. Primitive Gelasian, mentioned above, of which no manuscript exists. It is very probable that it has been lost for ever.
2. The Vatican manuscript *Reginensis lat. 316.* (Some pages are missing; these are in the Bibliothèque Nationale in Paris.)

[6] A. Chavasse, *Le Sacramentaire Gélasien* (*Vaticanus Reginensis 316*) (Paris, 1957). See especially, for the conclusion of this masterly study, pp. 679–92.

3. The Gallican manuscripts: Sacramentary of Gellone (*c.* 770); Sacramentary of Angoulême (*c.* 800); Sacramentary of Saint-Gall (800–20); Sacramentary of Rheinau (beginning of ninth century).

The Gregorian Sacramentary

It is necessary to mention the Gregorian Sacramentary before we consider the use made of the Gelasian and the influence that it exerted on the Roman Missal. The Gregorian Sacramentary is by far the most important of all because, with certain modifications and revisions taken from the Gelasian Sacramentary, it became the basis of our modern Missal.

The theory has been put forward—in the absence of evidence it is difficult to be more precise—that the Leonine Sacramentary was merely a collection of materials made in view of the compilation of a definitive Roman Sacramentary (that is, the Gelasian) and that towards the end of the sixth century St Gregory prescribed the compilation of a better arranged and more convenient Sacramentary. The variable prayers of the Mass, hitherto more numerous, were reduced to three, collect, secret and postcommunion, and a like reduction was made in the number of prefaces, *Communicantes* and *Hanc igitur* formulas.[7] The canon of the Mass here assumed its final form.

The manuscripts that we possess of the Gregorian Sacramentary (the earliest seems to be *c.* 790–816) all belong to the period of the expansion of the Roman rite throughout the West and it is in terms of this expansion that we can consider the manuscripts of the Gregorian Sacramentary. Pepin III's attempt to achieve liturgical uniformity within

---

[7] The earlier Sacramentaries, the Leonine especially, contained an abundance of optional formulas: thus there were twenty-eight proper Masses for St Peter, eight for Christmas and as many as 267 prefaces (beginning *Vere dignum*) in the incomplete Leonine Sacramentary that has survived. The Gelasian Sacramentary contained a mere fifty-four prefaces and *Hanc igitur* formulas.

his realms led to the adoption of the old Gelasian, subsequently modified with the admixture of Gelasian, Gregorian
and old Gallican texts; of this the chief manuscript representatives are those of Angoulême and Saint-Gall.

This attempt at uniformity can hardly have been successful,
for Charlemagne shortly afterwards felt obliged to begin anew
and obtained from Pope Adrian a copy of the papal Sacramentary. This book (known to liturgists as the *Hadrianum*)
was incomplete and did not contain the ordinary Sunday
Masses since it was a festival Sacramentary; it represented,
moreover, a developed form of the Gregorian reform. It contained however a short introduction which is precious in
that it shows us the shape of the Mass at the end of the
ninth century. This introductory section, entitled *Qualiter
missa Romana celebratur,* set out the various prayers and
chants of the rite from the introit down to the end of the
canon.[8] This manuscript of the end of the eighth century
displays almost entirely the elements of the Roman Mass
order of the time of St Gregory; the *Agnus Dei* inserted at
the end of the seventh century under Sergius is the only
addition.

The Gregorian Sacramentary was revised towards the
middle of the seventh century to include the Masses of
ordinary Sundays and those other days not included in
the *Hadrianum.*[9] This recension is known to us principally
through a manuscript of the chapter library at Padua and
consequently bears the name of *Paduense.*

Finally, we come to the revision of the Gregorian Sacramentary made by Alcuin. Charlemagne intended to enforce

[8] The *Gloria in excelsis* is ordered to be said on Sundays and
feasts, but only if the celebrant is a bishop. Exceptionally, priests
were allowed to include it on Easter day. The offertory is followed
by the prayer over the offerings (our secret prayer): *deinde offertorium
et dicitur oratio super oblatam.*

[9] The *Hadrianum* was a copy of the papal recension of the
Gregorian Sacramentary and included therefore only those days on
which the pope presided in person, that is the days of the stations,
still marked in our Missal, and some few days of the sanctoral.

the Roman liturgy throughout his dominions but to do this required the help of men of learning to supervise and effect the reform. The man for the work was to hand at the court. Alcuin (c. 735–804) was educated at his native York at the cathedral school of which he became master in 766. He encountered Charlemagne at Parma in 781, becoming his adviser in religious matters; later, as abbot of Tours, he established there an important school and library; there, too, he had under him pupils like Rhabanus Maurus and Amalarius who also have earned their niche in liturgical history.

Alcuin's problem was first and foremost to provide the emperor with the authentic Roman liturgy and to do this he had to complete the Sacramentary sent by Adrian. He distinguished the elements in that book that could not possibly go back to St Gregory,[10] effected changes in the canon (probably taking Gelasian readings as his authority)[11] and then proceeded to add in a supplement what was missing from the *Hadrianum*, drawing on complete recensions of the Gregorian that had penetrated over the Alps before the *Hadrianum* itself. He preserved certain local usages, adapted certain rites to local circumstances but seems to have preserved the Roman lectionary and chant (the antiphonary) almost intact. Alcuin's work is an example of liturgical development deserving of nothing but praise. The same cannot be said of his immediate followers nor of the work of those who transformed the Roman liturgy in the course of the next few centuries. But a different mentality was at work and a different conception of liturgy.

[10] For example certain Masses of our Lady, certain Masses in Lent and the Mass in honour of St Gregory himself.

[11] Thus the Gregorian Sacramentary, being a papal book, did not contain *et antistite nostro,* "for our bishop"; this was added by Alcuin as was the phrase *et omnibus orthodoxis* which refers to the bishops in union with the pope. The phrase is probably a reading from the old Gelasian inserted originally during the great doctrinal controversies of the fourth–fifth centuries when the maintenance of orthodoxy and the inclusion of a bishop's name in the diptychs were closely connected.

THE ORDINES ROMANI

The position by the middle of the tenth century can be summed up as follows. The Roman liturgy had been transported across the Alps and had taken root in the monasteries on the banks of the Rhine where it had undergone a certain transformation. With Alcuin's additions the form of the Mass had assumed its definitive shape. By being written down the forms of prayer had been fixed, the ritual gestures, the ceremonies, were known and handed on through practical experience. But when the Roman rite spread to the whole of the West and it became necessary to instruct those who had hitherto used other liturgies some sort of guidance was necessary for the ceremonies of Mass, the administration of the sacraments and so on. This guidance was provided by the *Ordines Romani,* the first of which was intended as an accompaniment in Gaul of the Gelasian and Gregorian Sacramentaries.

The most important of these *Ordines* is the first, *Ordo Romanus Primus,*[12] which, although the manuscripts are of a later date, describe for us the Mass as it was shortly after the time of St Gregory. Some points of importance emerge from a reading of this description. The first is that though in its principal features this solemn pontifical Mass is obviously on the same pattern as that in the Roman Missal today there are nevertheless certain elements for which we shall look in vain: there are no prayers at the foot of the altar, no prayers of offering (*Suscipe, Offerimus,* etc.), but once the gifts are on the altar the celebrant says over them

[12] Mgr Andrieu's great work on the *Ordines* has cleared up a great many doubtful points. He shows that Ordo I was sent from Rome "in about 750" at the latest and seems to have been drawn up in Rome towards the end of the seventh century. There is an edition of this *Ordo* with English translation which, though out of date on many points, is still valuable, by E. G. Cuthbert Atchley: *Ordo Romanus Primus* (London, 1905). I have not given here the description of the solemn Easter Mass from this *Ordo* as it is already to be found in this series in Amiot, *op. cit.,* pp. 21–6.

what we now call the secret prayer. Then the preface and
canon followed. Another outstanding feature of the solemn
Mass of the *Ordo Romanus Primus* is to be seen in the
processions—the imposing entrance procession to the strains
of the introit with the psalm sung *in extenso,* the procession
of clergy and people at the offertory and again at the communion.

The *Ordines Romani* date from the seventh to the fourteenth centuries and form a complement to the liturgical
texts, but the most important of them is the first.

The apologiae

Before the ninth century the Sacramentaries contained
solely the celebrant's part of the Mass—the collect, prayer
over the offering (secret) and postcommunion together with
the canon. From the ninth century onwards we begin to
find various prayers inserted for the private devotion of
the celebrant, prayers of penitence, confessions, professions
of humility. Some books contain a choice of formulas of
this kind. These various prayers appeared first of all in
collections intended for private use by monks and lay people
and from there they were incorporated into the Sacramentaries. In our present Missal the vesting prayers, the prayers
at the foot of the altar, incensing prayers, offertory prayers,
prayers before communion, *Placeat* at the end of Mass were
originally all private prayers of devotion. In fact all in the
Mass, save the canon, that is not said aloud belongs to this
category.

With the reorganization of the Church in Rome under
the German emperors in the second half of the tenth century,
and with the help of the reformed Benedictine monasteries,
the Romano-Frankish liturgy as it had evolved on the banks
of the Rhine and throughout the empire was introduced into
Rome itself, where it predominated. Simultaneously can be
observed the emergence of the "plenary Missals", complete
Missals, that is, with the whole text of the Mass (the cele-

brant's part and that of the other ministers) needed of course
for the celebration of low Mass, which at this time was becoming increasingly prevalent, with the result eventually that
the practice at low Mass began to invade that of high Mass,
and it grew common for the celebrant to recite the parts of
the other ministers.

It would be a mistake to see in this adoption of the
Romano-Frankish liturgy in Rome the signal for uniformity
throughout the West. While the pattern of the Mass rite
contained in the local Missals, which at this time began
to proliferate, was the same throughout the West many of
the details differed from place to place. Those prayers
particularly which had originated as *apologiae* and had been
inserted in the *ordo Missae,* first as private prayers then as
part of the rite, show great variations according to locality.

THE LATER MIDDLE AGES

The religious Orders with centralized forms of government
which appeared in the twelfth–thirteenth centuries felt the
need for liturgical uniformity and to this can be attributed
the eventual emergence of the rites of the Carthusians,
Cistercians and Premonstratensians. At a slightly later date
the Dominicans achieved liturgical uniformity. The Franciscans did likewise, choosing the liturgical books as reformed
by Innocent III for the use of the Roman curia; in this
Mass *ordo* will be found the prayers at the beginning of
Mass, the offertory prayers, prayers before communion, etc.,
much as we have them in the modern Missal.[13] The adoption
of these books by the Franciscans popularized them to a

[13] Comparison of this Mass *ordo* with the usual customs prevalent
north of the Alps at this time shows that the latter displayed greater
restraint. The comparison may be made easily enough by comparing
at the present time the prayers in question as they are in the modern
Roman Missal with the corresponding ones in the modern Dominican
or Carthusian Missals or as they are to be found in the Sarum
Missal (of which a printed edition is available).

great extent, and through the influence of these friars they were spread throughout Europe and even further afield.

It was the Missal of the curia adopted by the Franciscans and by them modified in some details which was imposed on the diocese of Rome by Nicholas III in 1277 and which became the Roman Missal as we know it today; in its present form it goes back then at least to the thirteenth century and represents a judicious choice from among the many plenary Missals of the Middle Ages.

THE REFORM OF ST PIUS V

The first printed "Roman" Missal was that which was published at Milan in 1474: *Ordo missalis secundum consuetudinem Romanae curie.*[14] In the order of Mass there are few differences from that of the modern Roman Missal. The time was ripe for liturgical reform. The exuberance of the local variations of the Roman rite with their many sequences and all sorts of customs, many of them strange and eclectic, had lasted long enough. The Council of Trent decreed the reform of the Roman rite and appointed a commission to deal with the matter consisting of Cardinal Bernardine Scotti, Thomas Goldwell (an Englishman and last Catholic bishop of St Asaph), Cardinal William Sirleto, Julius Poggi and others. The Council closed on December 4th, 1563, before the commission had finished its task and the matter was remitted to the pope, Pius IV. He died before the work was concluded and it was only under his successor, St Pius V, that the Missal resulting from the Council was promulgated. This is the Missal now in use.

The sources drawn on particularly by the commission of revision were the Missal of 1474 mentioned above and that of John Burchard of 1502; both contained the Mass

[14] The Henry Bradshaw Society has published an edition of this Missal in two volumes edited by R. Lippe (London, 1899), volume 17 of the publications of the HBS.

order of the Roman curia as adopted by the Franciscans in the thirteenth century. Burchard's Missal contained detailed rubrics compiled by him from the customs and practice that as master of ceremonies he had observed at the papal court. To all intents and purposes it was these rubrics and *ordo Missae* that was adopted by the commission appointed by Trent. St Pius V promulgated the new Missal by the Bull *Quo primum tempore* which is still to be found printed at the beginning of our modern Missals.

In the Mass propers the great number of sequences was reduced to the five we now have and a great many feasts of saints were deleted from the calendar.[15] Subsequent changes in this Missal have chiefly concerned the addition of further Mass propers. In view of the prevailing mentality and conditions in the sixteenth century the commission appointed by the Council of Trent probably did the best that it could achieve under the circumstances though nowadays we can regret some of the practices that it seemed to encourage and some of the matters that it did not make clear.[16]

[15] The calendar is dealt with below under Breviary.

[16] Recent reforms of the Missal and the events leading up to them are mentioned in the last chapter of this book.

CHAPTER II

THE ROMAN BREVIARY

"The canonical Hours of the Divine Office are directed by their composition to the sanctification of the different hours of the natural day" (*Rubrics of the Roman Breviary*, n. 142). Thus the Office is the Church's prayer for the sanctification of time. Nowadays it is found in the Breviary and its recitation in choir or in private is one of the obligations of clerics in major orders and of solemnly professed religious. But though now largely recited in private it is still the public prayer of the Church and most of the rubrics in the Breviary seem to assume that the Offices are celebrated in choir. To see how this prayer of the Church became, so to say, an institution carefully regulated by authority and imposed as a serious obligation on certain of the members of the Church we have to examine its evolution and some of its constituent elements.

ORIGIN AND CONSTITUTION OF THE OFFICE

In dealing with the history of the Office it is difficult to go back with any certainty beyond the eighth–ninth centuries. It is true that we can point to certain elements of the Office as being in existence at an earlier date just as we can discern from the documents of the primitive Church evidence for the existence of some form of public prayer, distinct from the Eucharist. But to say exactly what form this prayer took and to distinguish it clearly from private prayer is no easy matter, and to speak of an Office, that is, of prayer in common under the regulation of ecclesiastical authority, before the fourth century is, really, to go beyond the evidence. Of course, we can discover all sorts of indications that point to the subsequent formation of an Office, allow us to see the principles on which it was constructed and reveal its constituent elements.

Already in the Acts of the Apostles (3.1 and 10.9) we find references to prayer at the ninth hour and at noon and also (in 2. 42) to "fixed times of prayer". St Paul (in 1 Cor. 14. 28) refers to meetings for public prayer and in two other places (Ephes. 5. 19 and Col. 3. 16) seems to emphasize the community nature of this prayer. In the second century Pliny the Younger (in *c.* A.D. 112) tells us that Christians were accustomed to meet together on a certain fixed day before dawn and to sing a hymn to Christ as God.

In the third century the evidence begins to grow more plentiful. Tertullian speaks of morning and evening prayers as *legitimae orationes,* that is, an established custom regularly practised by the Christian community, in other words liturgical prayer. Clement of Alexandria and St Cyprian confirm this. Cyprian, indeed, seems to imply that this morning and evening prayer is a recently introduced practice. At Rome Hippolytus (in *The Apostolic Tradition*) shows us the Roman practice of the third century:

> All the faithful, men and women, directly they wake in the morning, before undertaking anything else, should wash their hands and pray to God.
> However, if there is to be a sermon, they should give preference to that ... for having prayed thus in the assembly we shall be strengthened against any evil the day may bring. ... If you are at home at the third hour, you should pray to God and offer him praise. If you are not at home, pray to God in your heart, for it is the hour at which Christ was nailed to the cross. ... In the same manner, you should pray at the sixth hour, thinking of Christ hanging on the cross

while the sun was checked in its course and darkness reigned. ... At the ninth hour your prayer and praise should be prolonged in imitation of the prayer of the righteous who praise God who is true to his promise.... Pray also before you lie down to rest. Towards the middle of the night arise again, wash your hands with water and pray.... About cockcrow get up again and pray once more.[1]

Hippolytus also gives a prayer for the blessing of the lamp at sunset. This evening prayer was of Jewish origin and consisted at first in a prayer of thanksgiving to which was added, in the Apostolic Constitutions, one or more psalms, a diaconal admonition, a prayer in litany form, a hymn and a final blessing. There seems little doubt that this form of evening prayer was the origin of our Vespers.

We have seen from the extract from Hippolytus above that prayer was counselled at the third, sixth and ninth hours (Terce, Sext and None) but it does not appear that these were any more than private prayers since they lacked the essential public character that would make them liturgical. Nonetheless, the other characteristic of the Breviary Hours is already apparent: Christians were urged to sanctify the different times of the day according to a fixed scheme.

This seems to have been the position up to the peace of the Church (313), though it is possible that the daily morning (Lauds) and evening (Vespers) office had already developed and was widely practised. The primitive Church, until the definitive emergence of official liturgies, seems not to have known any other public meetings for worship than those for the Eucharist, the vigils of the martyrs' anniversaries, the solemn Easter vigil and certain ill-defined, almost informal, meetings for prayer and preaching.

According to Eusebius and Denis of Alexandria, at the beginning of the third century Christian worship was largely

---

[1] The whole passage translated into English may be found in *Early Christian Prayers*, edited by A. Hamman, O.F.M., translated by Walter Mitchell (London and Chicago, 1961), pp. 253–5.

made up of hymns and canticles of Christian origin, but because of the errors contained in some of them and the dangers of Gnosticism they were given up and the Psalms substituted instead. Of these Christian compositions very little has survived: the *Gloria in excelsis* (sung in the East at the morning Office) and the φῶς ἱλαρόν (*Lumen hilare*) together with the *Te Deum* (though this is of slightly later date) are practically all that remain. The readings were taken from the Old and New Testaments, letters from other Christian communities, the acts of the martyrs. There was no idea of reading whole books of the Bible or the whole Bible within a specified time. As Dom Salmon remarks pertinently, "systematic reading of all the books of the Bible is only meaningful in the context of a daily Office" of the kind that the monks evolved at a later date.[2] Passages were chosen, on the contrary, as appropriate to certain occasions. The prayers at these meetings were in the first place the Lord's Prayer and then the collect. This latter was originally improvised before assuming a fixed form in the same way as the prayers at the Eucharist.

With the Peace of Constantine in 313 and the more systematic organization of worship the function of the clergy in connection with the public prayer began to be clarified; gradually they assumed the rôle that they have since occupied, that of representatives of the whole Christian body, deputed by the Church to offer praise and prayer to God for the needs of all.

MONASTIC INFLUENCES

From the third century onwards references to the Offices in the morning and in the evening become frequent; they are to be found in the works of Ambrose, Augustine, Hilary and Paulinus. The morning Office consisted of psalms, hymns

[2] See A. G. Martimort (editor), *L'Église en Prière* (Paris, 1961), p. 800.

and prayers, and special emphasis seems to have been laid on Pss. 148–50; by the fifth century there were five psalms, a canticle, versicles (known subsequently as *preces*) and the Lord's Prayer. The evening Office, or at least the form it assumed, grew out of the beginning of the Easter vigil with its blessing of the candle (the *lucernarium*) and the singing of psalms (Ps. 140 especially); by the fifth century this Office had been adopted for other days and soon became a daily practice leading up to Vespers. But there seem to have been no other occasions on which an Office was celebrated; there was certainly no question of public prayers during the day or of a daily vigil. The Easter vigil, and possibly those held before certain important feast days, were the only ones known.

The practice of a daily vigil came from the East through the influence of the ascetics. This is particularly clear from the well-known description of liturgical practice in Jerusalem at the end of the fourth century written by Etheria. The prayer of the ascetics at the various hours was private in nature though made in common; its liturgical nature arose from the fact of the participation of the clergy when they presided at it. It was especially in the East, also, that the monastic life developed and with this development came the organization of the Hours of prayer, the arrangement of the psalmody on a pattern that permitted its integral recitation within a specified period of time—anything between a single day and a fortnight. The principal innovation of the monks was the introduction of prayer during the night leading up to the morning prayer which has already been mentioned as characteristic of the Church at this period. In this way monastic and ecclesiastical practice were connected.

This is not the place to examine in detail the organization of the monastic Office as it developed in the course of a century and a half. It will be sufficient to say that by the end of the fifth century the monks were bound to a complete Office every day from vigils during the night (later known as Matins), Lauds, Terce, Sext, None and Vespers; to this series of Hours they had added Prime (after Lauds before beginning the work of the day) and Compline (night or dormitory prayers before retiring). On the other hand, in the parochial and cathedral churches the Christian community of the locality, under the presidency of the bishop or priest, was in possession of a simpler Office—the ancient Hours of morning and evening prayer (Lauds and Vespers). The monastic Office was distinguished by its emphasis on recitation of the Psalter within a certain period of time whereas the ecclesiastical Office possessed a greater variety of antiphons, collects and responsories. The monastic Office was more complete, the secular, parochial or cathedral Office was simpler (only two Hours) but more varied.

The influence of the monastic on the secular Office occurred principally through those churches, the Roman basilicas especially, where a community of monks existed to carry out the Office and a body of clergy to administer the sacraments. When the practice of making monks bishops became common it was not really remarkable that they tended to introduce their own monastic practices into the churches under their care. The sixth century contains many examples of this sort of things. St Caesarius († 542) ordered the singing of Terce, Sext and None daily in his cathedral at Arles; at Auxerre daily vigils were inaugurated at this period and the Council of Tours (567) called on all churches to adopt a *cursus* comprising Matins, Sext and Vespers (the Matins probably referred to the morning Office—Lauds—rather than to a vigil service). But it was in Rome especially that the influence of the monastic Office on the secular is to be seen to greatest effect; it was from a fusion of the two, the ancient Roman form and that laid down in the Rule of St Benedict, that emerged the form of prayer, the Divine Office, that prevailed throughout the West.

But it was a fusion of the two and not exclusively the influence of the Benedictine Office on the Roman that produced what came to be the Roman Breviary. St Benedict says on more than one occasion that he is taking the Roman arrangement of the Psalter and completing it, just as at another time he says that he is lightening the burden of the older monastic rules by imposing a weekly recitation of the Psalter.

Just as the Roman Sacramentaries crossed the Alps and underwent revision at the hands of the Franco-German liturgists, finally making their way back in their new form to the place whence they had come, so too the books of the choir Office underwent the same process. By the middle of the ninth century this Office had achieved its highest point of perfection.

Amalarius of Metz (*c.* 780–851), Alcuin's pupil and admirer, despite his allegorism and sometimes absurd explanations, has left us an extraordinarily clear description of the Roman Office as it emerged from its Carolingian transformation. From Amalarius' two works (*De Ordine Antiphonarii* and *De Ecclesiasticis Officiis*) we can reconstruct the main elements of this Office.[3]

THE OFFICE IN THE NINTH CENTURY

All the Hours began with the Lord's Prayer said privately to which was added at Matins and Prime the Apostles' Creed.[4]

Matins

The Office began with *Domine labia mea aperies* followed immediately by *Gloria Patri,* then came Ps. 94 (*Venite exsultemus*) with its refrain (invitatory) recited in the ancient manner known as responsorial, that is, with each verse followed by the antiphon. After the invitatory and psalm came

[3] Both these treatises have been reprinted in Migne's *Patrologia Latina* volume 105, columns 1243 following. (The *Patrologia Latina* is hereafter quoted as *P.L.* followed by volume and column number.)

[4] This was the prescription of St Benedict of Aniane († 821), the monastic reformer. The *Ave Maria* was a later addition and in any case the prayer did not at that time exist in the form in which we have it now.

the hymn. This is prescribed in the Rule of St Benedict where he speaks of it as *Ambrosianum,* meaning possibly a hymn after the manner of St Ambrose, or one written by him or even perhaps sung in the fashion of the Church at Milan. Hymns were not received in the Office of the Church in Rome itself until the twelfth century but were usual in the monasteries and churches in Italy and elsewhere in Europe. The psalms followed: eighteen on Sundays (twelve in the first nocturn, three in the second and third) and twelve (in one nocturn) on weekdays. The psalms at Matins began with Ps. 1 on Sundays and went straight through the Psalter to Ps. 108 as the last psalm on Saturdays. The Psalter was said right through in the week; Pss. 109–50 were said at the day Hours.

After the psalms of Matins came the lessons (on Sundays and feast days three after each nocturn's psalms): Isaias was read in Advent; from Christmas to Septuagesima the other prophets; from Septuagesima until Easter the Pentateuch, Josue, Judges; from Easter to Pentecost, the Acts and the Catholic Epistles, the Apocalypse; during the summer the books of Kings and Chronicles; from autumn to December the sapiential books, Job, Tobias, Esther, Judith, Esdras, Machabees. For the most part this is the order still followed nowadays.

Each lesson was followed by a responsory which can best be described as being in the same form as the gradual at Mass. The *Gloria Patri* was said at each responsory (not at the last of each nocturn as nowadays) and there were often two, three or more verses.[5]

The ferial nocturn contained twelve psalms which were followed by three lessons and three responsories. Amalarius does not mention the *Te Deum* at Matins. In many churches it followed the ninth responsory; when it was adopted at

[5] An example of a responsory on the old pattern may be found in the modern Breviary on the first Sunday of Advent, first responsory, *Aspiciens a longe.*

Rome it took the place of this responsory. On Sundays the second and third nocturn lessons were taken from the writings of the Fathers and (in the third nocturn, sometimes) from St Paul's Epistles. In those days the whole Office was not to be found within the covers of one book and a great many volumes were required, especially for the lessons, though not very much later a lectionary was composed, together with a homily book.

Lauds

Lauds could not begin before sunrise. After *Deus in adjutorium*, etc., and *Gloria Patri* there followed four psalms and a canticle; the last psalm was always Pss. 148–50 regarded as one. After the psalms came a short lesson (called nowadays the little chapter), a hymn in those places which admitted hymns, a versicle and response, the *Benedictus* and the collect. The general pattern was very much the same as nowadays.

Prime

Prime also followed in general arrangement its pattern in the modern Roman Breviary, that is to say, after the introductory *Deus in adjutorium*, etc., and the hymn (*Jam lucis orto sidere*) three psalms were said. Amalarius mentions Ps. 53 and two portions (of sixteen verses) of Ps. 118. At a later date Ps. 117 was substituted as the first psalm for Sunday Prime, and the Athanasian creed (*Quicumque vult*) was also added, on Sunday only in some places, every day in certain churches in Gaul. The collect for Prime (*Domine Deus omnipotens*) asking for help throughout the day was probably written by Alcuin or else found by him in some Sacramentary that has since been lost. For some centuries Prime concluded with this collect; all that nowadays follows (reading of the Martyrology and the "chapter" prayers which come after it) is of monastic origin.[6]

[6] See below, chapter III, for further details about the origin of the Martyrology.

Terce, Sext, None

These three Hours have remained practically as arranged by St Benedict, though the Roman as distinct from the monastic Office appoints three portions each of sixteen verses of Ps. 118 at each Hour daily; the monastic Office spreads Ps. 118 over Sunday and Monday (thus requiring three portions of eight verses each at the different Hours) and makes use of the gradual psalms on the other days. Terce, Sext and None concluded with the little chapter, Kyrie and Lord's Prayer. Amalarius does not mention the collect. The hymns said at the beginning of these hours were the same as those in the modern Breviary, though in some places variants were appointed at certain seasons of the year, for example in Lent.

Vespers

After the introductory versicles Vespers had five psalms taken from the series 109–47, little chapter, hymn, versicle, Magnificat with antiphon, Kyrie, *preces* and collect.

Compline

The order was that followed in the Breviary before the reform of St Pius X (1911), that is with Pss. 4, 30. 1–6, 90, 133 daily. The hymn was usually that still in use (*Te lucis ante terminum*) but at certain seasons of the year others were substituted in some places (for example, *Christe qui lux es et dies* during Lent or winter).

ADDITIONS TO THE ROMAN OFFICE

Basically the Office described above was a simple one and though longer than that now current in the Church was not notably longer than the Breviary Office before St Pius X's reform. But it very soon grew very much longer than it has been now for some hundreds of years. In the first place there

was a tendency for the lessons at Matins to be lengthy.
The lessons as described in Amalarius' work quoted above
were certainly longer than those of the modern Breviary
but certainly not so long as the form adopted in the tenth–
eleventh centuries in many churches in imitation of the
practice at Cluny. There they were very long indeed.

Ulric, an eleventh-century monk of Cluny, has left us some
account of the liturgical practices there in his day and in
particular of the length of the lessons:

> To begin with the most ancient of all books, that is, the
> Octateuch: this book is appointed to be read in Septuagesima.
> ... On the Sunday itself, there are but short lessons; except
> that, for the first, the whole of the prologue *Desiderii mei* is
> read. During the following nights the lessons are so much
> increased that in one week the whole book of Genesis is
> gone through in the church. On Sexagesima, Exodus is begun,
> and together with the other books which are read, it is also
> read both in the church and in the refectory ... and the whole
> Octateuch is read through, if not before, by the beginning
> of Lent. ... As the nights grow shorter so do the lessons.
> Care must however be taken that they are not so abbreviated
> as not to allow sufficient time for the brother who goes the
> round ... with his dark lantern to see if anyone has gone to
> sleep during the lesson. ...
>
> From the calends of November the lessons for common
> nights are doubled. The prophet Ezechiel is appointed to be
> read in the church only and is customarily finished before
> the feast of St Martin. ... In Advent, Isaias the prophet is
> appointed and when I inquired about this, and wished to
> learn in how many nights it ought in strictness to be read
> through I could not learn from anybody, and I can only say
> what I recollect to have heard and seen. When I was there
> it was sometimes read through in six common nights.[7]

Examination of this extract reveals the length of the lessons
at Cluny: St Jerome's prologue *Desiderii mei* (still printed
at the beginning of the Vulgate) is as long as about eight

[7] Ulric, *Consuetudines*, cap. 1, *P.L.* 149, col. 643 *et seq.*

average Scripture lessons in the modern Breviary and this
was the first of the (four) "short" lessons on the night of
Septuagesima; Genesis contains fifty chapters; at a little
over seven chapters a night they could just manage to get
it read by Sexagesima. And these, it must be remembered
were the lessons of the first nocturn, for at the other nocturns
the lessons were taken from the Fathers.

The exaggeratedly long lessons were not the only factor
that made the Office wearisomely lengthy. As early as the
end of the eighth century, at first in the monasteries under
the influence of Benedict of Aniane († 821) and then elsewhere, other prayers and Offices were added. These additions
were some of them matters of private devotion but subsequently, and fairly rapidly, they became of obligation.
Additions of this kind were the Office of the Dead, the Little
Office of the Blessed Virgin, the seven penitential psalms,
the fifteen gradual psalms, the litany of the saints. In monasteries and cathedral choirs were added certain extra psalms
(the *psalmi familiares*) after the Hours of the Office, psalms,
that is, said for the good estate of living benefactors or
the repose of the souls of those who had died. All these
things caused a great lengthening of the Office whose effects
were to be seen in the following centuries. Perhaps things
were worse in this respect at Cluny than elsewhere—in the
course of a single day 138 psalms were recited in the church,
though not necessarily by all the monks—but the length of
the Office at Cîteaux, for example, according to modern
standards must have been long enough—the monks there
said the Little Office and the Office of the Dead almost daily
—and Cîteaux, it will be remembered, was to some extent
a reaction against the liturgical practices of Cluny.

THE OBLIGATION OF THE OFFICE

Originally there seems to have been no question of the
clergy being obliged to the Office personally; the primitive

morning and evening Offices were regarded as the prayer of the local Church in which its members participated according to their order. For monks, presence at their longer and more complete Office was of obligation as can be seen in Cassian, for example, by the punishments laid down for those who arrived at it late. In the smaller churches it does not seem that there was a daily Office; it was celebrated according to the opportunities and needs of the congregation, perhaps only on a Sunday. In cities, the Office seems in part to have been celebrated in different churches in turn; none of them enjoyed the complete daily Office. We have to await the eighth century and the reform of the clergy and liturgy that took place to witness the emergence of the idea of obligation in a definitive form. And then the emphasis was more strongly on the celebration of the Office in church. St Chrodegang of Metz († 766), whose name is important in the history of the canonical life, drew up a rule for his clergy grouping them round the church to which they were attached and obliging them to the complete daily Office. He seems to have envisaged some sort of obligation of supplying in private what for a legitimate reason a cleric could not perform in public. Several of Charlemagne's prescriptions and those of the Council of Aachen (816) insisted on the obligation for all clerics of taking part in the full daily Office of their church and, though there was no mention of their making up in private what they could not perform in public, the idea that they were bound to do so began to gain ground about this time.[8]

[8] There could be no question of course of a cleric absent from choir saying privately the same Office as that which he had missed. To do so he would have needed a number of bulky books, though he was supposed to know the psalter by heart. In those days those who supplied in private what they had missed in public did so by reciting certain psalms and prayers known by heart. Monastic rules give directions to a monk showing how he was to supply, on a journey for example, the Office at which he could not be present. We have to wait some centuries yet before the idea of saying in private an Office identical with that missed in choir became general.

THE REFORMS OF ST GREGORY VII
AND INNOCENT III

By the beginning of the eleventh century the Roman Office, while at the day Hours remaining very much as it has been described above, at Matins exhibited the following forms: on Sundays, three nocturns of eighteen psalms in all and nine lessons, on ferial days one nocturn of twelve psalms and three lessons; on feast days three nocturns each of three psalms and three lessons; finally the Easter Office, to which that of Pentecost and its octave were very soon assimilated, of three psalms and three lessons. Some clerics, tempted by the shortness of the Easter Office, had endeavoured to introduce a Matins for the whole year with only three psalms and three lessons. St Gregory VII in 1074 ordered that Matins throughout the year should follow the pattern as hitherto observed. Innocent III's contribution to Breviary history was greater. He codified and corrected the Office of the Lateran basilica adapting it to the needs of the pontifical court and it was from this reform that came the "Office of the curia" or the *Officium modernum* as it was called. The officials of the papal court who celebrated the Divine Office in a chapel in the papal palace obviously could not carry out the elaborate ceremonies such as were celebrated in the great Roman basilicas and other large churches. Nor on their frequent journeys could they carry about with them the whole library of books necessary for the Office. Previously, more or less successfully, attempts had been made to enclose within the covers of a single volume the whole of the Office, but the resultant books were heavy volumes still only suitable for choir use. The Breviary of the Roman Curia as it evolved in these circumstances was a portable book containing the Office for the whole year. Its handier format was achieved by abbreviation of the Scripture and patristic lessons and by indicating the psalms by their opening words rather than by writing them all out in full (churchmen were still supposed to know the Psalter by heart).

It was this Breviary that was adopted by the Franciscans and propagated by them as they spread all over the then known world; and because of their exceedingly rapid expansion this Breviary of the Curia soon made its mark. But not only did the Franciscans adopt the Breviary of the curia, they refashioned it to suit their own needs and, approved by Gregory IX in 1227, it was made obligatory for all the churches of Rome by Nicholas III (1277–80). While this Romano-Franciscan Breviary was obviously the direct descendant of the old Roman Office several elements of the ancient antiphonary disappeared from it; at the same time most dioceses and religious Orders preserved elements of the old Roman Office that had been given up in Rome itself. (This was the case, for example, with the Premonstratensians.) Haymo of Faversham († 1244) was responsible for the revision of the Breviary of the Curia as it had been adopted by the Franciscans; Benedict XII made it obligatory in Avignon in 1337; finally Gregory XI imposed it at the Lateran (1370–8).

The whole spiritual movement which found its principal expression in the Franciscan Order exerted a powerful influence on the Office, not always, it must be said, a wholly beneficent one: new feasts were introduced in such numbers that finally the Office of the season was considerably dislocated and frequently neglected to make room for the celebration of the Offices of the saints. The lessons from the Bible and the Fathers were abbreviated not only for the purpose of achieving a portable handy volume but also because the devotional tendencies of the times were somewhat out of harmony with these elements, though it is true that one motive for the favour accorded to the Offices of the Sanctoral was the desire to avoid the lengthy additional prayers and Offices obligatory when the ferial Office was said.

Consider the Office on a ferial day in the fourteenth

century. The fifteen gradual psalms and the Matins and Lauds of the Little Office of our Lady preceded the Matins of the day, which itself consisted of twelve psalms and three lessons; at Lauds, before the collect, long ferial *preces* (which included Ps. 50) were said and the Office was followed by Lauds of the Dead; in Lent, in addition, the seven penitential psalms would have to be said. At Prime, again long ferial *preces* and Prime of the Little Office of our Lady; each of the other Hours of the day was preceded by the corresponding Hour of the Little Office. At Vespers, also preceded by Vespers of the Little Office, long *preces* as at Lauds were said before the collect, and Vespers of the Dead followed. Compline was preceded by one nocturn (three psalms and three lessons) of the Office of the Dead and followed by Compline of the Little Office. There can be small wonder that churchmen tended to favour the introduction of feasts of saints which at one stroke relieved them of the obligation of all these extras to the Office of the day. Then, too, the Sunday Office was very long, with its eighteen psalms at Matins and long Prime; the substitution of an Office from the sanctoral with nine familiar (because constantly recurring) psalms and nine short lessons (very often all from the legend of the saint) was an advantage that could be contrived to be of frequent occurrence by the introduction of new feasts.

The calendar of the Breviary as it continued to develop, with an increasingly diminishing emphasis on the proper Office of the season in favour of the proper of the saints, was the cause of a revolution in the nature of the Office, but the contents of the Breviary itself were by no means above reproach. Much spurious matter was introduced; although in view of the state of knowledge of the period perceptive historical criticism is not to be expected it is symptomatic of the changed view of the Office that many of the "historical" lessons (that is, the legend) of the saints (some Offices had six, some all nine lessons from the legend) were taken from apocryphal sources condemned by the *Decretum Gelasianum*[9] or from spurious "acts" of the martyrs filled with incredible events like those of St George, St Catherine and St Barbara.

By the end of the thirteenth century the rule that clerics were bound to private recitation of the Office when they could not go to choir was becoming widely accepted and the fact that the choral Office could thus be omitted in favour of its private recitation led gradually to a certain shift of emphasis. Though all down the Middle Ages and indeed up to the time of the French Revolution the Divine Office was celebrated in monastic, cathedral, collegiate and parish churches it was increasingly regarded as a clerical activity, and while of course in theory it remained the prayer of the whole Church, in practice it was envisaged rather as a prayer of the clergy.

Salimbenus in the second half of the thirteenth century criticizes the Breviary Office. He writes that it is

not yet well set in order according to what many would wish, nor indeed really and truly; for many superfluous things remain, which are a greater cause of weariness than of devotion, both to those who hear the Office and to those who say it. Such is the long Sunday Prime when the priests ought to be saying their Masses and the people are waiting for them and there is none to celebrate: he is busy saying his Prime. So, to say eighteen psalms in the Sunday nocturn Office or ever you come to *Te Deum,* and that just as much in the summer when the fleas are troublesome and the nights are short and the heat intense as in the winter is nought but a weariness. There are many other things in the ecclesiastical Office which might well be changed for the better, and should be, of right; for they are full of barbarisms though all men do not perceive it.[10]

[9] If, as seems probable, this decree did not emanate from the pope whose name it bears, it belongs at least to the early sixth century.
[10] Quoted in Pierre Batiffol, *History of the Roman Breviary* (London, 1898), p. 211.

The four seasonal antiphons of the Blessed Virgin were added during the thirteenth century and the prevalence of private recitation called for the addition of some rubrics of a more detailed nature than had hitherto been necessary. This form of the Office, which had emerged in the thirteenth century, was to endure practically to the end of the sixteenth century and its broad pattern is still to be discerned clearly in the modern Roman Breviary. But even by the end of the thirteenth century, or at all events shortly afterwards, the time was ripe for a thoroughgoing reform. Council after Council deplores the coldness of the clergy in reciting the canonical Office, even in choir. They do not, Mgr Batiffol points out, "sufficiently recognize the fact that this coldness, this scandalous negligence, proceeds in part from the deterioration of the Office itself . . .". And he adds:

> To sum up, how far have we got from the broad and harmonious simplicity of the Roman Office of the eighth century! The antiphonary and the responsorial, the *ordo psallendi* and the *ordo legendi* of old are preserved, and the hymnal is added; but the lectionary is become scanty and very corrupt. And if we owe a just debt of gratitude to those who gave us the antiphons of the Blessed Virgin, what are we to say, on the other hand, of the additional daily offices? It is difficult not to see in these additions, these numerous and burdensome services of adventitious prayer, a grave wrong done to the canonical Office itself. The grand and simple lines of the edifice remain, but a huge number of parasitical little chapels block off the nave and aisles.[11]

Because Mgr Batiffol made a mistake about the origin of the Office of the Roman curia a recent work on the Franciscan Breviary[12] takes him to task for quoting with approval Ralph de Rivo, the fourteenth-century canon of Windesheim, who blamed the Friars Minor for the unsatis-

[11] *Op. cit.*, pp. 225–6.
[12] S. J. P. van Dijk, O.F.M. and J. Hazelden Walker, *The Origins of the Modern Roman Liturgy* (London and Westminster, Md, 1960).

factory state of the Office. Yet it is beginning to be seen nowadays that the Franciscan approach to the public worship of the Church, at least as it appears in their medieval liturgical books, constituted an innovation that the reform currently in progress is endeavouring to remedy. And Ralph was surely right when he reproached the Franciscans with having multiplied saints' days of nine lessons in order to avoid the ferial Office and the obligation of reciting the penitential and gradual psalms and the Office of the Dead.

THE REFORM OF THE COUNCIL OF TRENT

In the fourteenth and fifteenth centuries there were constant demands from Councils, provincial synods and ecclesiastical authorities for greater fervour in the celebration of the Divine Office. There seems to have been little realization that part of the evil was to be found in the form of the Office itself. Diocesan Breviaries proliferated, all of them based on the Roman *ordo psallendi* and many of them preserving elements of the old Roman Office that had disappeared from the "modern Office" propagated by the Roman curia and the Franciscans. Thus the ancient Easter Vespers with the procession to the font remained in many Breviaries long after it had been given up in Rome. Nevertheless, a state of liturgical anarchy prevailed, particularly in the local calendars: all sorts of feasts and popular observances found their way into the worship of the Church and some of them at least were utterly unsuitable.

With the invention of printing the evil grew worse; reform was urgently necessary and the more enlightened churchmen looked to Rome to achieve it by a General Council. Meanwhile there were individual attempts at reform in the early sixteenth century, some of which were inspired by the Renaissance then in its infancy; the results can hardly be termed happy.

Leo X entrusted Zacharias Ferreri, bishop of Guardia

Alfiera, with a revision of the Breviary; he announced his intention of producing "an ecclesiastical Breviary made much much shorter and more convenient, and purged of all mistakes" (*breviarium ecclesiasticum longe brevius et facilius redditum, et ab omni errore purgatum*). A start was made by the issue of a new hymnal as a sample of the good things to come; it was published with papal approval on February 1st, 1525. In his introduction to the work Ferreri castigated the barbarisms to be found in the hymns of the Office, but in trying to apply the rules of classical Latin poetry to Christian hymns he produced compositions that appeared laboured in comparison with the original hymns of which he disapproved so strongly.[13] But what is to be urged against Ferreri principally is not that he produced a pastiche of classical Latin with excessive mythological allusions in the place of Christian hymns, but that he totally misunderstood the nature of the Office. Fortunately, his projected Breviary

[13] For those who wish to compare Ferreri's efforts with the compositions that he abhorred the following examples are offered. Thus the first strophe of the *Veni Creator Spiritus* becomes:

> Xenophanis ceu Lesbii,
> Te iambicis attolimus
> Concentibus; sic effice
> Nos esse caelis compotes.

A more original composition is the hymn for Lent:

> Bacchus abscedat, Venus ingemiscat
> Nec iocis ultra locus est, nec escis,
> Nec maritali thalamo, nec ulli
>   Ebrietati.

> Clauditur ventri ingluvies voraci,
> Clauditur linguae labium loquaci,
> Jamque de verbis abigunt salaces
>   Series nugas.

Yet his spirited hymn for the Common of Apostles shows that he was capable of producing something better:

> Gaudete, mundi principes,
> Quorum fide et constantia
> Et supplici innocentia
> Sunt victa regum culmina.

disappeared in the sack of Rome (1527) and nothing more was heard of it. Clement VII had approved Ferreri's hymns and authorized their use in the Office. He now turned to Quignonez, a Franciscan and a cardinal, entrusting him with the preparation of a new Breviary which, to quote the introduction of the book when it appeared, should "arrange the canonical Hours, bringing them back so far as possible to their ancient form, to remove from the Office prolixities and difficulties". It was to be faithful to the institutions of the ancient Fathers and the clergy were to have no longer any reason for revolting against the duty of reciting the canonical prayers. Quignonez' Breviary was published in 1535 and approved by Paul III for private recitation by priests occupied in study or exceptionally busy with other work.

This new Breviary arranged the Office on an entirely new plan. The psalms were distributed over the days of the week in such a way that the whole psalter was gone through in a week; there were three psalms at each Hour and no psalm was said twice in the course of a week, but the same psalms were said every week, proper psalms were never appointed, so that on a Friday, for example, the same psalms were said whether it was Christmas Day, Good Friday or the feast of an apostle. There were three lessons at Matins, the first of which was taken from the Old Testament, the second from the New and the third from the Fathers or the legends of the saints. Quignonez adopted a critical attitude to the legends and by a more extended use of Scripture (the Scripture lessons were longer than was then the custom) endeavoured to make the Office an instrument of instruction for the priest rather than the prayer of the Church. It was intended for private recitation and therefore its compiler confined it to psalms, antiphons and lessons—there were no little chapters, versicles or responsories. The collects were those customarily in use.

Although this Breviary was intended for private recitation

it very soon spread to some cathedral choirs, particularly in Spain where at Saragossa there was almost a riot on Maundy Thursday when the congregation, unable to recognize their usual *Tenebrae,* set about the canons of the cathedral who had adopted the new Office. Despite the widespread success of this new Breviary it was repudiated finally at the Council of Trent.

The reform of the Breviary figured on the agenda of the Council and various projects were put forward. The twenty-fifth session left the matter of liturgical reform in the hands of the pope; a commission was appointed under Pius IV and worked at the production of a reformed Breviary and Missal; the task was continued under St Pius V and brought to a successful conclusion with the publication of the reformed Roman Breviary to which was prefixed the Bull, *Quod a nobis* (July 9th, 1568).

By this Bull the Quignonez Breviary was definitely abolished and all others also which could not show a pre-scription of two hundred years. This would have saved most of the local Breviaries but many dioceses and some religious Orders did not take advantage of the opportunity of retain-ing their own Breviaries and adopted the Roman; others reformed their own books on the lines of the new Roman one.

The principal changes were to be found in the calendar which was lightened by the suppression of a certain number of feasts and octaves leaving thus some 200 days in the year free for the ferial Office. To make this latter more attractive the supplementary Offices and psalms that hitherto had accompanied it were generally abolished. The psalter re-tained the ancient distribution of the psalms and the Gallican version was made obligatory. Sunday Prime was shortened and the patristic and hagiographic lessons were revised and corrected.

Together with these changes in the text of the Breviary it is important to notice also a changed attitude to the Office that had been growing up over the course of the previous centuries. The new Tridentine Breviary did not mention private recitation of the Office, but henceforward the emphasis seems to be almost entirely on private recitation. The choral Office came to be regarded almost as a monastic practice and the spiritual movements of the sixteenth and seventeenth centuries, by making men concentrate on the practices of a "devout life" and personal perfection, even reacted against the choral Office as a distraction to the private prayer of the priest. The French school of spirituality emphasized still more strongly the suitability of private recitation as a priestly obligation, even as a priestly devotion intimately connected with the reception of Orders. "The celebration of the Office, regarded as the prayer of the Church, had always been at the same time the priest's personal prayer; henceforward the former gave way to the latter." [14]

THE BREVIARY FROM THE END OF THE SIXTEENTH CENTURY TO THE END OF THE NINETEENTH

The Tridentine Breviary as it was published under St Pius V remained in use down to 1911, but during the intervening period certain changes were made in it. Many of the feasts abolished by St Pius V were reinstated in the course of the next hundred years (for example, the Presentation, St Anne, St Francis of Paula, St Anthony of Padua, St Nicholas of Tolentino). Urban VIII caused certain lessons to be corrected and instituted a number of feasts of saints, but a more serious modification was that made in the text of the hymns. A commission of four Jesuits was entrusted with the correction of the hymns of the Breviary in accordance with the rules of classical prosody. In reality they deformed the work of Christian antiquity as can be seen by comparing the

[14] Dom Salmon, *La Prière de l'Église*, p. 849.

hymns in their old version with those in the modern Breviary.[15]
After Urban VIII, Clement X (1670–6) added many more
feasts to the calendar (most of them doubles—in occurrence
with the Sunday Office they thus superseded it).

The neo-Gallican Breviaries

Meanwhile attempts were made elsewhere to achieve a
further reform of the Breviary Office. In France many
churches, taking advantage of the clause in *Quod a nobis*,
had retained their own Breviaries, carrying out certain changes
in the light of the new Roman book. In 1680 François de
Harlay, archbishop of Paris, produced a revised Breviary
for his diocese and Claude de Vert did so for the Cluniac
Benedictines. Both these reforms, though effecting many
changes in the lectionary and responsorial, were in the main
traditional. About half a century later came a further reform
of the Paris Breviary; it was the work of Grancolas and
Foinard and was issued under the authority of de Vintimille,
the archbishop. Here the changes were far more radical,
many of Quignonez' ideas were adopted and a new distribution of the psalter was made. The longer psalms were split
up and varying psalms were appointed for the Little Hours
throughout the week, a scheme that was adopted in the reform of the Roman Breviary under St Pius X in 1911. This
new Paris Breviary set the fashion for changes on the same
lines in many of the dioceses of France, Germany and Austria
and by the time of the Revolution most of them were using
a Breviary that was in no sense a reform of their former
one but a completely new creation. In addition to the novel
distribution of the psalter two other general principles were
applied in the compilation of these Breviaries: the first was
a great sobriety in the calendar; there were far fewer feasts

[15] The old versions can be found in the monastic, Carthusian,
Cistercian, Dominican and Carmelite Breviaries at the present day.
One of the worst examples is furnished by what was done to the
hymn of the dedication Office. On this subject see J. Connelly,
Hymns of the Roman Liturgy (London and New York, 1957).

so that the Office of the season was not superseded[16] and, save for the hymns, "ecclesiastical compositions" were deleted in favour of texts taken from Scripture. The principle was a mistaken one for from the beginning in addition to Scripture there have been ecclesiastical compositions in the liturgy and an examination of these new Offices in comparison with the Roman Breviary shows clearly the superiority of the latter in this respect: the new Breviaries display an intolerable pedantry. This is particularly true of the responsories. The hymns too were rewritten; it cannot be said that they were serious rivals to the old Roman hymns.[17]

It has been urged that many of these Breviaries exhibited Gallican and Jansenist characteristics. That they contained passages that could be interpreted in this sense is certainly true and it is a pity because for this reason they have been condemned out of hand by many when the principles underlying the composition of these books were, in fact, generally sound. That this is so may be seen by comparing these Breviaries with all the recent reforms of the Roman Breviary, in which, it will be noticed, the very same principles have been applied. The chief defect of the French Breviaries was that they were changed and promulgated without reference to the Holy See and in defiance of the liturgical law prevailing at the time.

Benedict XIV's projected reform

During the nineteenth-century controversy in France on the subject of the diocesan Breviaries nothing was known of the project of reforming the Roman Breviary that had been entertained and worked upon by Benedict XIV. He

[16] No feasts were allowed to be celebrated in Lent, a rule that with some modifications has been adopted in the latest recension of the Roman Breviary.
[17] Santeuil was the author of many of the Paris hymns. Polemists have objected that he was not even a priest though one can hardly understand what that had to do with it; it is hardly likely that ordination would have made him a better hymnographer.

was well aware that certain of the complaints against the Roman Breviary were well founded and set up a commission to study the question giving it as its terms of reference two documents, one French and the other Italian, that he had received on this subject. Both called for the reform of the calendar, legends and other elements, but the French document demanded also a new distribution of the Psalter while the Italian was for retaining the Breviary of St Pius V. The commission could not agree on this last proposal and confined itself to dealing with the calendar. It called for the suppression of a great number of feasts. The feast of the Holy Name, the Name of Mary, the Rosary, our Lady of Ransom, our Lady of Mount Carmel, the Seven Sorrows, the translation of the Holy House of Loretto and others were all to go, together with ninety feasts of saints, among them Gregory VII, Aloysius, Antoninus, Raymond of Pennafort, Casimir, Vincent Ferrer, Francis Borgia; a number of saints' feasts were to be reduced in rank from double to simple and the celebration of saints in Lent was to be forbidden. Of the legends many were suppressed altogether and others were corrected. Some fifty new lessons were provided in place of those held to be spurious.

This revision took six years to achieve and, seeing the temper of the times, was unlikely to meet with approval. Consequently the pope shelved the project to enable him to study it further; unfortunately he died in 1758 before he was able to do anything about it. It is interesting to notice that many of the things complained about in the reformed French Breviaries were contemplated in this scheme and that certain of its recommendations have been carried into effect in recent years.

The nineteenth century

The battle waged by Dom Guéranger against the illegitimate Breviaries led to their final suppression during the course of the nineteenth century; in France and Germany one diocese after another returned to the Roman liturgy. Unfortunately in doing so they lost also certain legitimate elements of their ancient liturgical heritage which might well have been preserved. The last diocese to adopt the Roman Breviary was that of Paris in 1873.

Projects for the reform of the Breviary were put forward at the Vatican Council (1870) but were not reached before it broke up. Leo XIII in his turn set up a commission to study the question but little came from this save the rule that lesser feasts should not be transferred when they were in occurrence with another, thus leaving a few extra days free for the ferial Office. In the course of the three centuries or so since St Pius V's reform the calendar had again become so overloaded that the Offices of saints now almost entirely superseded the liturgy of the season: the Sundays of Lent and Advent, Christmas, Holy Week, Easter and Whitsun were almost the only relics of the liturgical year that were still celebrated. The ferial days of Advent and Lent (save for Ash Wednesday), the Sundays after Epiphany, Easter and Pentecost in practice disappeared from the calendar since they were all at the mercy of any occurring double feast or to some feast assigned to a particular Sunday as its fixed day.[18] Sacristans, since the green vestments were never used, had them dyed another colour and priests had their Breviaries bound up without the ferial psalter.

Many new Offices were added to the Breviary under Pius IX and Leo XIII. The latter, having made the rule about the transference of certain lesser feasts, thus leaving a few days free for the ferial Office, proceeded to fill in the gaps by giving permission for votive Offices on free days of the week. The new Offices seem all to have been written with private recitation in mind and most of the hymns of this

---

[18] Thus the Sundays of October were all occupied by feasts of our Lady: the first Sunday, feast of the Rosary, the second, the Maternity of our Lady, the third, the Purity of our Lady, the fourth her Patronage.

period, it seems curious to state, were not written to be sung.[19]

This then was the position at the end of the nineteenth century; liturgical anarchy was as great in many ways as just before the Council of Trent and reform was urgently needed. The beginning of the twentieth century saw the first steps towards this reform which is still in course of being carried out.[20]

[19] One of the worst examples of unsuitable hymns is that in the Office of the Sacred Heart by an unknown eighteenth-century writer. It contains, for example, the following verses:

> Ex corde scisso Ecclesia
> Christo jugata nascitur.
> Hoc ostium arcae in latere est
> Genti ad salutem positum.
>
> Decus Parenti et Filio
> Sanctoque sit Spiritui,
> Quibus potestas gloriae
> Regnumque in omne est saeculum.

One commentator has been so bold as to compare the author of these hymns to St Ambrose. It hardly seems likely that St Ambrose could have produced lines like those above.

[20] Its principal stages are briefly described below in chapter VI.

CHAPTER III

THE MARTYROLOGY

At the end of Prime in the Roman Breviary occurs a rubric directing that at this point in choir the Martyrology is to be read and adding that it is praiseworthy to do so when the Office is said in private. The Martyrology is a catalogue of the saints in which they are classified according to the day of their death (their *dies natalis,* that is, their heavenly birthday) and the place where they died. Thus, on each day of the year there is an entry commemorating the saints who died on that day, each entry beginning with a place name. The first entry daily is of the saint whose Office is said on that day.[1] It is followed by the other saints whose *dies natalis* occurs on that day. From very early times catalogues of the martyrs were compiled, first of the martyrs of a locality and then of those of neighbouring Churches also, finally the names of confessors and holy virgins were added. A history of the Martyrology, then, would amount to a history of the cultus and veneration of the saints in the Church and would lie outside the scope of this short study. But to understand the evolution of the Martyrology certain elements of this history must be treated here.

---

[1] For example the first entry for October 15th reads: *Abulae in Hispania, sanctae Teresiae Virginis, quae Fratrum ac Sororum Ordinis Carmelitarum arctioris observantiae mater exstitit et magistra.* "At Avila in Spain, St Teresa, Virgin, who was mother and mistress of the Brothers and Sisters of the Carmelite Order of stricter observance."

GENESIS OF THE MARTYROLOGY

In pagan antiquity the dead were commemorated and in continuing to commemorate those who had died for their faith in Christ the early Christians in one sense perpetuated a characteristic tradition, but with this difference: the pagans commemorated their dead on their birthdays but the Christians celebrated the day of their deaths, the *depositio,* but kept the name: τὰ γενέθλια, *dies natalis,* for the day of death or burial. The anniversary of St Polycarp is an example of such a commemoration in the primitive Church; it was instituted at Smyrna immediately after his death: his bones were reverently gathered together and the account proceeds: "We laid them in a place befitting them. May the Lord grant us to meet again there when in gladness and joy we can celebrate the anniversary day of his martyrdom. . . ." The cultus of the martyrs in the early Church consisted essentially in the gathering of the Christian community around the tomb to celebrate the Eucharist on the *dies natalis.* Tertullian regards this custom as established in his day and St Cyprian († 258) calls on his priests to note carefully the day of a martyr's death.

At the end of the fourth century a canon of the Council of Hippo (393) shows that on a martyr's anniversary the *acta* (that is, the account of his martyrdom) were read at the Office. At an earlier date than this it appears that there were catalogues in existence at Rome and that notaries were appointed by the popes to keep them. Such catalogues amounted to local Martyrologies. In the first place they contained, as we have seen above, the anniversaries of the martyrs. Then, possibly in the third century, the anniversaries of bishops were added; next came the dedication of churches and the translation of relics that took place on these occasions; finally, in the early fifth century, the names of benefactors of churches and of those holy people (the ascetics) who confessed their faith by their penance as the martyrs did by their blood.

The most ancient local Martyrologies known are the catalogue of Dionysius Philocalus (354)[2] which mentions the anniversaries of twelve popes and twenty-four martyrs, and the calendar of Carthage (fifth–sixth centuries). The latter places anniversaries of martyrs and bishops together: *hic continentur dies nataliciorum martyrum et depositiones episcoporum quos ecclesia Carthaginiensis anniversaria celebrat.* The year begins after Easter and finishes on the 13th of the calends of March (February 17th). No feasts are given for Lent. Together with African saints are several of Rome, Italy and the East. The compilation represents the transition from local martyrologies to general.

GENERAL MARTYROLOGIES

What have been called above the local Martyrologies were in fact little more than calendars of local saints. The general Martyrologies collect together the names of a certain number of saints whose anniversaries fall on the same day but without regard to their local celebration. It was towards the middle of the fifth century that the first martyrology in the proper sense of the word was compiled. Because its preface places it under the patronage of St Jerome it is known as the Hieronymian Martyrology. It is the basic document for hagiographical studies.[3] The manuscripts (the most ancient of which go back to the eighth century) all depend on a Gallican version made at Auxerre in 592, but its primitive state can be fairly easily reconstructed. Its three principal sources appear to have been the Roman calendar of 354

[2] Fuller details of this will be found in Noële M. Denis-Boulet, *The Christian Calendar* in this series, pp. 52 following.

[3] There is a fine critical edition by H. Delehaye: *Commentarius perpetuus in Martyrologium Hieronymianum ad recensionem H. Quentin* (Brussels, 1931). This book forms the second part of the Bollandists' *Acta Sanctorum Novembris II.*

mentioned above, the Antioch calendar (the *Breviarium syriacum*) and an African calendar of which the Carthage calendar represents a later version. Like the older calendars, the *Hieronymianum* generally confines its entries to mention of the day of the anniversary, the place and the saint's name. Occasionally it adds a line or two about the circumstances attending the martyrdom of certain saints.

The *Hieronymianum* attained importance before the fuller "historical Martyrologies" were in circulation; these, as we shall see later, were drawn up to provide something more than a mere list of martyrs. But the importance of the *Hieronymianum* in the context of this short study of the history of the Martyrology is to examine the purpose for which the book was used, and a revealing clue to this is given by the manuscripts in which it is to be found. Of the forty or so manuscripts that are known fifteen of them occur in conjunction with the Rule of St Benedict, five of them are to be found with a Sacramentary. Both of these facts show, it would seem, a probable monastic or liturgical use; and it appears that the Martyrology was used at first for the announcement by the deacon of the Roman stational Mass and afterwards when, as in Gaul, there was no question of a stational Mass, for the announcement of the next feast day.[4]

In the eighth century certain legislative texts make quite clear that the Martyrology was used in church or in chapter. The English Council of Clovesho in 747[5] lays down (in

[4] The evidence for this statement may be found conveniently in Mgr Andrieu's *Les Ordines Romani du haut moyen âge*, volumes II (Louvain, 1948) and III (Louvain, 1951). For example Ordo XVII describing a Mass in a Frankish monastery tells us that the deacon announces the *natalicia sanctorum* "occurring in that week as follows: on the coming day of week is the anniversary (*natale*) of holy Mary, or of a confessor or of some other saint according to the Martyrology. And all answer *Deo gratias*" (vol. III, p. 183). The feasts for the week were announced, then, *qualis evenit secundum martirilogium*.

[5] Though we know of the canons of this and other Councils of Clovesho its situation is unknown; it has been identified with Abingdon and with Cliff near Rochester, but without sufficient reason.

canon 13) that the festivals of the saints are to be observed throughout the year on the same day according to the "Martyrology of the same Roman Church". Since there was then no Roman book of the sort in existence the canon refers probably to a copy of the *Hieronymianum*. A more important canon is the sixty-ninth of the Council of Aachen which prescribes that at chapter "the Martyrology is read in the first place, then is said the versicle concluding the silence [that is, the monastic great silence between Compline and Prime], the rule or some homily is read and lastly *Tu autem Domine* is said". A final quotation may be made from the fourth recension of the Rule of St Chrodegang for canons regular where, concerning Prime, it is laid down that "after the lesson the age of the month and moon are given out and the names of those saints whose feasts occur on the morrow and afterwards is said the verse 'Precious in the sight of the Lord is the death of his saints' ".[6] There are many other synodal decrees and monastic customaries in the same sense that could be quoted.[7]

THE HISTORICAL MARTYROLOGIES

All these decisions of Councils and monastic legislation were responsible not only for a proliferation of copies of *Hieronymianum*, but of a new kind of Martyrology which has been given the name "historical" because it relates the circumstances of the saint's life in addition to the essential details of place and date of martyrdom. One of the first, if not the first, was that by the Venerable Bede (*c.* 673–735); it is possibly based on a previous historical Martyrology, though this is conjecture without supporting evidence. Bede's book was composed at the beginning of the eighth century; in his Ecclesiastical History he writes: "A Martyrology of the birth-

[6] *P.L.* 89, 1067.
[7] For example, the *Regularis Concordia*; see the edition by Dom Thomas Symons (Edinburgh, 1953), pp. 17, 28.

days of the holy martyrs: in which I have been at pains
diligently to set down all whom I could find and not only on
what day, but also by what manner of contest and under what
judge they overcame the world."[8]

Bede's Martyrology begins on January 1st and contains
114 historical notices and a certain number of short entries;
about 180 days are left vacant. His sources seem to have
been primarily the *Hieronymianum*, fifty passions of martyrs
and a round dozen of ecclesiastical writers among whom are
Eusebius, St Jerome, St Gregory of Tours and the *Liber
Pontificalis*. He is careful about dates, generally following
the *Hieronymianum* and displays the scholarly concern that
usually characterizes his work. But because he did not give
a notice for every day in the year his work could not entirely
supersede the *Hieronymianum* and he was quickly followed
by other writers who utilized his work to a greater or lesser
degree, without always following his learned caution in leaving
a day blank when there was nothing to place against it.

Bede, therefore, started a fashion and he was followed
by other compilers some of whom form links in the direct
line from him to the modern Roman Martyrology, while
others appear as offshoots in this genealogical table. Two
such offshoots are the compilations by Rhabanus Maurus
(† 856) and that known as Pseudo-Florus to distinguish it
from the genuine work of Florus, the deacon of Lyons. Here
we can confine our attention to the direct sources of the
Roman Martyrology, though in passing it will not be without
interest to note the existence of a metrical Martyrology claim-
ing Bede as its author. It was not written by Bede, but its
eighty-three hexameters are certainly of English origin and
came probably from Ripon or York.

A direct descendant of Bede is the manuscript (which
we may call Bede II) of his Martyrology containing the

---

[8] *Historia Ecclesiastica* V, 24 (Plummer's edn., 1, p. 359); the
translation quoted above is that made at Louvain by Thomas Stapleton in the sixteenth century (new edn, London, 1935, p. 336).

mention of the death of St Boniface and his companions (754); this became the typical version of the Bede Martyrology. Towards the end of the eighth century, or the beginning of the ninth, various short notices were added from an eighth-century Gelasian Sacramentary to a manuscript of this family of the Bede Martyrology (this therefore becomes Bede III). In the first half of the ninth century we find a Lyons Martyrology which develops Bede's notices and adds French and especially Lyonnese saints. Florus, a deacon of Lyons († *c.* 860) compiled a Martyrology from the above sources, completing them with historical and topographical notes which are generally valuable. Of this work there are two families of manuscripts (designated here as Florus I and Florus II). The Martyrology compiled by Florus was used in the composition of Martyrologies that were either contemporary with or a little later than his date, the principal authors of which that concern us here being Ado and Usuard.

Ado of Sens († 875), archbishop of Vienne, compiled a Martyrology at Lyons between 850 and 859, a book remarkable by the length of its notices (Ado I); there are two other families of manuscripts of this work (Ado II and Ado III) but they need not concern us here save to say that they represent both the full version (as in Ado I) and a shorter version of the same work. Ado's influence on the Roman Martyrology will appear in a moment but first a word must be said of Usuard.

He was a monk of Saint-Germain-des Prés. In about 875 he wrote to Charles the Bald that he had been led to establish a certain unity in the solemnities of the saints, making use for the purpose of various Martyrologies. Among these were the *Hieronymianum,* Bede, Florus (that is, more often than not, Ado's version of Florus). All previous collections seem to have been laid under contribution but Usuard added his own, filling up the blanks in the calendar (in his book there are 1170 names as against 800 in Ado), shortening some of the longer notices and adding various touches of his own. This Martyrology enjoyed great success; manuscripts of it are very plentiful and adaptations and abbreviations of the book followed one another all down the succeeding centuries.

Usuard, magpie-like, used, it seems, every source that came to hand but he relied directly on Ado I and on the other sources mentioned previously to which he had access through Florus II. If he had relied exclusively on Florus II his sources, though not unimpeachable, would have remained at least authentic to the extent that they were all historical documents and that Florus was a careful historian. But Usuard relied also, and perhaps to a greater extent, on Ado I and unfortunately it is impossible to say of Ado what was said above of Florus. Ado in fact is the villain of the piece who has exerted down the centuries an enduring and pernicious influence on all subsequent Martyrologies.

In his Martyrology are to be discerned various changes, the addition of details of all sorts, embellishments that seem to have been added to improve the story and to make his Martyrology outstanding and successful. The principal authority that he quotes in the preface to his book is an ancient Martyrology, sent in olden times by a pope to a holy bishop of Aquilea. This venerable document, Ado says, was lent to him by a monk for a few days when he was staying in Ravenna and he took advantage of the loan to make a copy of it. Now this *perantiquum Martyrologium* as he called it (known to posterity as the *Parvum Romanum*), is nothing else than a version of Florus II with additions by Ado himself. In other words, it is a forgery, and a forgery clever enough to have deceived many compilers of Martyrologies, including Baronius, down to the present day. Dom Henri Quentin, who proved that the *Parvum Romanum* was a forgery made by Ado to give authority to his own Martyrology, has this to say of Ado's influence on hagiography:

On almost every occasion, whenever the tradition of the Martyrologies has caused difficulties to historians, we have

encountered this author's hand. Whether it was a question
of Hippolytus of Antioch or of the Apology of Aristides and
of St Denis the Areopagite, of the peculiar dates given to
the feasts of St Ignatius or of the date that Baronius felt
justified in assigning to the ordination of St Basil, of the
origins of the festival of All Saints or the location at the
Latin Gate of the tradition of the cauldron of boiling oil in
connection with St John . . . , of the death of St Cecily under
Marcus Aurelius, of Anastasius of Salona, of the Four Crowned
Martyrs, of Christina of Bolsena, etc. . . . , it is always Ado's
testimony which is at the root of part if not of the whole
difficulty. Ado has exercised on the development of Martyrology literature the most unfortunate influence with the aggra-
vating circumstance that in order to endow his work with
authority superior to that of other Martyrologies compiled
at his own period he did not scruple to include in it the
alleged *venerabile perantiquum martyrologium romanum*,
which he was supposed to have relied on but of which he
was himself the author.[9]

Usuard's compilation spread rapidly and shortly before
the Council of Trent in one form or another was the Martyrology of almost every diocese and religious Order. The first
printed edition was that published at Lübeck in 1475. In
1498 an Augustinian friar, one Belinus, published a revision
of Usuard as the Martyrology of the Roman Curia. Despite
its title this was a publication made solely on Belinus'
authority, but it served as a basis for the revision of the
Martyrology after the Council of Trent. In pursuance of
the decrees of the Council Gregory XIII appointed a commission (Baronius was one of the members) to produce a
revised Martyrology; the ten members, basing their work on
Usuard and making use of Bede, a recently published menology
and the *Dialogues* of St Gregory, produced the *Martyrologium
Romanum ad novam kalendarii rationem et ecclesiasticae
historiae veritatem restitutum Gregorii XIII jussu editum*, but

[9] Dom Henri Quentin, *Les Martyrologes historiques du moyen âge*
(Paris, 1908), p. 678.

it had to wait for its third edition, published in 1584, to obtain papal approval. The editions of 1589 (Antwerp) and 1598 (Rome) had the benefit of certain revisions by Baronius.

SOURCES OF THE ROMAN MARTYROLOGY

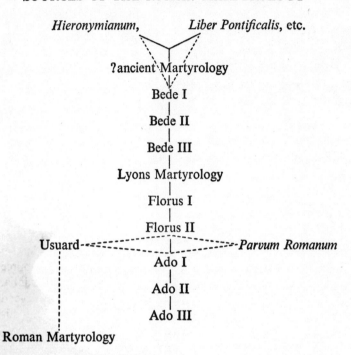

Benedict XIV revised the edition that had appeared under Urban VIII (1630) and explained the principles of his revision in the long letter still printed at the beginning of the Martyrology. The latest typical edition is that of St Pius X (1914) and the most recent edition that of 1956 (*quarta post typicam*) which, save for the addition of saints canonized since the previous edition, reproduces the *prima post typicam* approved by the Congregation of Rites on January 11th,

1922. It was this edition which was severely criticized by scholars and, since it is necessary at this point to say something of the present text of the Martyrology, the nature of these criticisms will have to be examined.

THE PRESENT STATE OF THE MARTYROLOGY

"For long past a correction of the Martyrology has been desired in the Church," wrote Dom Henri Quentin[10] in reviewing the edition of 1922. From what we have seen in the summary history of the text of the Martyrology it can cause surprise to no one that the book is full of errors and though a great number of them can be imputed to Ado by no means all of them are his responsibility. Examination of the entry for November 27th, for example, reveals the existence of Saints Barlaam and Josaphat: "In the part of India bordering on Persia Saints Barlaam and Josaphat whose marvellous deeds were related by St John of Damascus." The marvellous deeds of these two legendary figures were not written by St John of Damascus and it has now been recognized that the whole story "is a purely imaginative romance about two saints who never existed, but its source is now recognized as being the legend of Siddartha Buddha. ..."[11] The adoption of an imaginative romance as the legend of a saint is not unknown in hagiography but how did this example of the practice gain entrance to the Martyrology? It was not in Bede, Florus or even Ado. In fact it was inserted by Baronius, who justified the entry by reference to a *Catalogus Sanctorum* by Pietro de' Natali (probably written in 1372) and to "other authors", by which he meant, probably, the supplements to Usuard made by Greven and Molanus, unofficial compilations dating from the end of the fifteenth

[10] *Analecta Bollandiana,* XLII (1924), p. 387.
[11] *Butler's Lives of the Saints* edited, revised and supplemented by Herbert Thurston and Donald Attwater (London, 1956), IV, p. 433.

and the early sixteenth centuries; their principal concern was to increase the length of their lists.

The example given above is not unique, though possibly it is more extreme than others; it has been quoted to show the sort of entry that requires deletion from the Martyrology. Errors of date, of place, confusions of names of persons with those of places have all been made, and again not only by the old compilers of Martyrologies but by their successors or revisors at a later date.

The editor of the edition of 1922 added errors of his own. Although the book was not published as a new edition but merely as *prima post typicam* (that is, of the typical edition of 1914) it is in reality a complete revision: "there are more differences between it and the *typica* of 1914 than between any of the typical editions and the *editio princeps* of Gregory XIII."[12] Dom Quentin reckoned that revisions of one sort or another had been made in 1500 to 1800 notices at least, but none of the glaring errors of the Martyrology or the spurious matter was eliminated and other errors were committed. The work had been begun under Benedict XV and the book was completed and published under Pius XI but he would not allow his name (it is customary for the reigning pope's name to appear on the editions of the liturgical books published during his pontificate) to be printed on the title page of so unscholarly a production. It appeared as approved by Benedict XV.

It is clear therefore that a radical reform of the Martyrology is long overdue. That Baronius and his assistants should have been unsuccessful in producing a really critical text will surprise no one who is aware of the means at their disposal in the sixteenth century. Nowadays, with all the work done by the Bollandists in the centuries since Baronius' time, and particularly with the essential works that they have produced in the last few decades,[13] the time

[12] Quentin, *art. cit.,* p. 392.

[13] In addition to the critical edition of the *Hieronymianum* mentioned above there is the whole series of studies (*subsidia hagiographica*) of great value and the *Propylaeum ad Acta Sanctorum*

is ripe for the production of a Martyrology that, excluding the spurious and erroneous features of the present book, should contain a list of the authentic saints of the Church.

The question has sometimes been raised as to what is the precise significance of the insertion of a name in the Roman Martyrology. Benedict XIV dealt with this point in his treatise *De Servorum Dei beatificatione et beatorum canonizatione,* book I, chapter 43, where he stated that the infallibility of the pontifical judgement is engaged by the insertion of the names of saints in the Roman Martyrology only in the case of those saints solemnly canonized by the Roman pontiffs, and he goes on to mention the insertion of other names, taking it for granted that such an insertion is an equipollent or otherwise formal beatification or canonization, and yet, in spite of that, he does not allow that the pontifical judgement is thereby involved. Dom Quentin sums up the matter admirably:

> Not only the pontifical authority but even the episcopal authorities have never intervened to guide the choice of compilers. The Council of Aachen in 817 ordered the reading of the Martyrology after the Office of Prime; episcopal statutes lay down that priests must have a Martyrology ... but the official decrees are confined to those matters and each compiler keeps his entire freedom in the choice of those things it is fitting to include in his work. Certainly, in many cases, the saint introduced in this way on private authority into the book is already in possession of a regular *cultus* ... but there are others again where the compiler's principal intention is to fill up as best he can a day that has remained empty and where he has no other source save an authority of no value. ... It is clear therefore that it would be as imprudent to rely blindly on the Roman Martyrology, the direct heir of the

---

Decembris (Brussels, 1940) which is a critical edition of the *Martyrologium Romanum* (1914 typical edn) with bibliographical and source references for each entry. With these works alone it would be possible to produce a Martyrology free from the glaring errors of the present book.

Middle Ages, as it would be temerarious to lay on the ecclesiastical authority responsibility for the errors that it contains.[14]

If the Martyrology is to continue to be read in the public worship of the Church—and there is little purpose nowadays when no one is without an ecclesiastical calendar or *Ordo recitandi* with which to organize the day's Office—it is surely urgent that its text should be free from glaring errors and spurious matter.

[14] Quentin, *op. cit.*, p. 689.

CHAPTER IV

THE PONTIFICAL AND
THE ROMAN RITUAL

THE PONTIFICAL

The history of the Pontifical as a separate book containing the rites and sacraments whose celebration and administration are reserved to the bishop begins in the tenth century; before that date the necessary formularies were to be found in the Sacramentaries, and the *Ordines* described the rites to be carried out. In other words, the sources of the Pontifical are the same as those of the Roman Missal. Little, therefore, need be said of this early stage of evolution of the Pontifical though in describing some of its rites it will be necessary to refer to their primitive form.[1] The Leonine Sacramentary, for instance, contains the Mass for the dedication of churches, the consecration of bishops, the ordination of priests and deacons, the consecration of virgins and the solemn blessing of marriages (*velatio nuptialis*); some of the fine consecratory prefaces of the modern Pontifical are already to be found in this Sacramentary. The Gelasian (Gellone) Sacramentary contains the forms for solemn baptism, confirmation, exorcisms, dedication of churches and consecration of sacred vessels all classed together; these are followed in a further section by the rites for the ordination of clerics, subdeacons,

---

[1] See above, pp. 13–21 and, in this series, F. Amiot, *op. cit.* and L. C. Sheppard, *op. cit.*, referred to on p. 11, note 3 and p. 13, note 1.

deacons and priests, the consecration of a bishop, the blessing of abbots and abbesses, monastic profession and the consecration of virgins; finally there are Masses for coronations
and the nuptial blessing. These rites all show developed
forms.

The Gregorian Sacramentary enables us to carry the story
a little further. Alcuin in his revision of the *Hadrianum* tells
us in the preface (*Hucusque*) that he had supplied the rites
for the minor orders; he also made additions to the rites
for the consecration of virgins, the dedication of churches,
coronations and exorcisms, taking them from the rites current
in Gaul at the time. Further additions were made after
Alcuin's time, and when the Roman Sacramentary thus em-
bellished made its way back to Rome it contained a great
many elements of foreign origin which were adopted in the
very centre of Catholicism.

The Sacramentary provided the text of the rites, the
directions were to be found in the *Ordines Romani* which
are pontifical in the fullest sense of the word because, originally at any rate, they seem only to envisage the pope as
celebrant of the rites that they describe. The Pontifical comes
to us in reality from a combination of elements in the Sacramentaries and in the *Ordines*. The first compilation which
included all pontifical functions can be dated between 950
and 962 and comes from the monastery of St Alban at Mainz,
though such works as the English so-called Pontifical of
Egbert and Benedictional of Robert[2] and one or two other
sporadic attempts of the same kind represent possibly a
contemporary tendency in the same direction. The Pontifical
of Mainz enjoyed a considerable vogue; copies of it were
made for the churches of Germany and Italy; in France, also,
many examples of it are to be found.

By the end of the tenth century the Pontifical of Mainz
had made its way to Rome, probably through the influence

[2] Editions of both of these have been published by the Surtees
Society and the Henry Bradshaw Society.

of the Ottos, the German emperors; the German provenance of these documents can often be detected by some small detail as, for example, when one of them gives an oath of obedience to the bishop of Salzburg. A certain amount of rearrangement took place, however, resulting in the inversion of the first and second parts. Previously the ceremonies of Lent and Holy Week, blessing of the oils, baptism and confirmation had come first, followed by ordinations, coronations, professions and blessings (of abbots, abbesses, etc.) and the consecration of churches. The new order was to put in the first place:

Ordinations (major and minor orders);
coronations of emperors;
blessings of abbots, abbesses, virgins;
monastic profession;
consecration of churches.

Then in the second part were to be found:

Ceremonies of Lent and Holy Week;
blessing of the oils;
baptism and confirmation;
ordo of penitents (in place of the Lenten one);
visitation of the sick;
extreme unction;
liturgy of the dead.

This was the order, with some modifications, that was adopted in the Roman Pontifical.

We now encounter a name that has made its mark in liturgical history. William Durandus (1230–96) was a canonist and a legal official of the Roman curia; he became bishop of Mende in 1285, and attended Gregory X at the second Council of Lyons, the decrees of which he drafted. He is best known perhaps for his *Rationale divinorum officiorum*, a kind of "inquire within upon everything" liturgical, a book whose influence has not been for the best in the history of Christian worship. Dom Cabrol says of it that "it is principally a compilation of previous studies with a mystical commentary in which the author gives exaggerated importance to symbolical interpretations. His principles, which led astray some authors in the nineteenth century, need to be received with caution." But it is his version of the Pontifical which concerns us here.

In the *Rationale* he mentions the Pontifical which he had drawn up (*in libro Pontificali per nos edito*) and which was published in about 1292. That Durandus was a canonist can be seen in the arrangement of his Pontifical; his tidy legal mind had already done the same thing with his *Rationale* which is in eight books covering the whole of his subject-matter under neat categories—things, persons, vestments etc. His edition of the Pontifical is consequently divided into three parts, the first dealing with persons, the second with objects and the third with various rites (of the liturgical year) and ceremonies.

Durandus' purpose, then, while respecting tradition and without innovating, was to arrange the Pontifical as an authentic liturgical book reserved to the use of bishops; consequently he omitted from it baptism, penance, extreme unction and matrimony because these sacraments are not, as he tells us, exclusively administered by bishops. At once on publication it became authoritative; as early as the beginning of the fourteenth century Clement V (1305–14) referred to it as an authentic liturgical document. Nevertheless, it seems difficult to assign a precise date for its definitive adoption by Rome though it is certain that it was widely used elsewhere in the West; Dom Puniet points out that in 1389 an archbishop of Arles possessed a *Pontificale secundum usum seu consuetudinem ecclesiae Romanae* in which Durandus' division into three books as above does not yet appear.

Nevertheless, by the fifteenth century it seems to have been definitively adopted, for Piccolomini, the revisor of the Roman Pontifical, states that in revising and editing the Pontifical he followed Durandus but without departing from the text and arrangement of the Roman Pontifical. He reproduces Durandus with certain additions.

Piccolomini, so called because he had been adopted by Aeneas Piccolomini, the future Pius II, was made bishop of Piacenza in 1484; previously he had been a papal master of ceremonies. From Piccolomini's preface to his work (in the form of a letter to Innocent VIII who had commissioned the work) it appears that the pope had instructed him to revise the text and produce a book that was to be made the authentic edition for the whole of the West. The principles that he adopted can be shortly summarized:

1. He omitted certain rites that had fallen into desuetude, like the expulsion of penitents on Ash Wednesday and their reconciliation on Maundy Thursday; he also omitted certain formulas that could also be used by priests, as Durandus had done.
2. He added from other books of the pontifical Curia certain formulas that were missing from Durandus, like the blessing of a knight, blessings of vestments, pyxes and reliquaries, the reception of princes and the pontifical blessing.
3. He added precise directions for pontifical ceremonial— when the bishop should wear his mitre, when he should stand, sit, etc.

Piccolomini's Pontifical was printed in Rome in 1485. In 1511 a new edition was published in Venice and Lyons with the title *Pontificale liber,* the first time that the title had occurred, though in the body of the book one still notices *Pontificalis ordinis liber* as hitherto. At the end of this edition are added the special pontifical blessings for Mass which are derived from Gallican usage. They have never been adopted at Rome. They were reprinted in a further edition of the Pontifical that appeared in Venice in 1520, though there is a note in the book stating that these blessings were not used in Rome.

This edition was the work of Alberto Castellani, O.P., who tells us that his principal concern was not to take away anything that Piccolomini had included in the Pontifical but rather to put back what former editors had rejected from the Pontifical of Durandus which, as he said, was redolent of sacred antiquity. One of Castellani's additions was unfortunate, to say the least, for it might well have affected the validity of some ordinations. With a view to preventing the ordination of the unworthy he inserted a protestation, to be read by the archdeacon in the bishop's name, that the bishop's intention in ordaining was confined to those who were not under censures of various kinds or who did not belong to certain categories; thus were excluded those who obtained ordination by simoniacal means. As Benedict XIV points out, such a practice could cause endless scruples and indeed the protestation was omitted from sub-sequent editions of the Pontifical though the fact that Benedict XIV thought it necessary to refer to it would seem to show that while the protestation had disappeared from the Ponti-fical it was still the practice of some bishops to make it at the diocesan synod where the effect would be the same.[3]

As a result of the labours of Castellani and his predecessors, by the time of the Council of Trent the Church was in possession of a Pontifical that had been revised by the order of the popes on more than one occasion, but it had never been given that formal approval that we are nowadays ac-customed to in the case of liturgical books. The Council of Trent had indeed laid down that the received and approved rites for the solemn administration of the sacraments were not to be departed from and made arrangements for the publication of authentic editions of the liturgical books. We have already seen the result of this in the case of the Roman Breviary and Missal. The Pontifical had to wait until prac-tically the end of the century for its authentic edition ac-

[3] The text of the protestation can be found in F. A. Zaccaria, *Bibliotheca Ritualia* (Rome, 1726), vol. I, p. lxiii.

cording to the rules of Trent, though editions were published in 1561 and in 1579, "emended by the authority of Pius IV" and "added to and emended according to the laws of the Council of Trent".

Writers about the Pontifical are accustomed to say that by the end of the sixteenth century there was an authentic Pontifical in existence which, though revised by papal order, did not yet enjoy their formal approval.[4] By this they mean that the popes, although they had been vigilant to see that a true and authentic text of the Pontifical was established, had not yet made this text of obligation on all bishops; it was still legal for a local Pontifical to be followed.

The process of liturgical centralization and uniformity set on foot by the Council of Trent developed fairly rapidly. In 1587 Sixtus V founded the Congregation for Sacred Rites and Ceremonies, entrusting it with the special duty of correcting the liturgical books: "that as the need arises they should reform and correct the books of sacred rites and ceremonies, in the first place, the Pontifical, Ritual and Ceremonial". That was as far as the project seems to have been taken under Sixtus V. Some fifteen years later Clement VIII revived his predecessor's scheme and appointed a special commission to study the documents and produce an official Pontifical. The basis of this reform was Castellani's edition of 1520; some mistakes in it were corrected and its general arrangement was tidied up, the rubrics were simplified and those which were purely ceremonial in character were relegated to a new book, the Ceremonial of Bishops. The book was promulgated (February 10th, 1596) by Clement's Constitution *Ex quo in Ecclesia Dei*, still printed at the beginning of the Pontifical. Its text merits examination for it discloses the principles followed in compiling this new edition. Clement VIII says that despite the efforts of his predecessors, who had taken care to endow the Church with an authentic

[4] For example, Dom P. de Puniet, *The Roman Pontifical, A History and a Commentary* (London, 1932), p. 49.

Pontifical, numerous errors had found their way even into
the formulas of the rites so that he had felt obliged to
appoint a commission of learned men to revise the text
of the Pontifical and bring it into agreement with the ancient
manuscripts and restore them to their former authentic state
lost through the carelessness of printers, or the erosion of
time or other causes.[5] But the greatest innovation was the
abolition of all local Pontificals absolutely, no account being
taken of the fact of their previous approbation or whether
they enjoyed a prescription of two hundred years or more
(as St Pius V had allowed in the case of Missal and Breviary).
The *Pontificale Romanum,* as its official name now became,
was, and has remained, obligatory on all bishops following
the Roman rite and its derivatives.

To all intents and purposes the history of the Pontifical
ends at this point; subsequent emendations down to 1961
have been of a very minor character and most of them hardly
merit mention, though it is perhaps useful to cite the editions
of Urban VIII and Benedict XIV. The former was printed
at the Vatican Press in 1645 with Urban VIII's name added
to the title page: *Pontificale Romanum Clementis VIII primum, nunc denuo Urbani VIII auctoritate recognitum.* The
rite of monastic profession was deleted but those for the
expulsion and reconciliation of penitents were put in, though
there is no record of their ever having been used. Certain
matters (the form for blessing or making a cantor—*de officio
Psalmistae*—the rite for the first cutting of a clerk's beard
and the *Scrutinium* formerly held on the evening before a
bishop's consecration) were relegated to the end of the
volume as customs of the Church no longer in use.

[5] His precise words are: *Ceterum, quia eaedem ceremoniarum, ac
rituum formulae ibi expressae, postea, sive diuturnitatis injuria, sive
Typographorum negligentia, sive alia de causa in ipso Pontificali
partim immutatae, partim corruptae, veteris instituti, atque auctoritatis
gratiam magna ex parte amiserant, idcirco necessaria res visa est, ut
eaedem formulae in sacris Praesulum Ecclesiasticorum muneribus
servandae, recuperato prioris integritatis statu, omnino restituerentur,
et ab omnibus, praescripta, firma aliqua ratione, observarentur....*

Benedict XIV ordered a reprinting of the Pontifical laying down quite clearly that no additions were to be made to the book, though he himself added the rubric that in confirmation the bishop was to lay his hand on the head of the candidate as he anointed his forehead.

TWO RITES IN THE PONTIFICAL

There can be no question here of examining all the rites of the Pontifical, tracing the history of their development and assigning a date for the introduction of each element in its developed form. Elsewhere in this series will be found something about the evolution of the rites of ordination[6]; here it will be useful to examine shortly the evolution of the two episcopal rites that are more commonly encountered: confirmation and the dedication of churches.

Confirmation

The first rite set out in the Roman Pontifical is that of confirmation, thus showing its dependence on the Pontifical of Durandus who excluded from his compilation all rites that were not the exclusive function of bishops. Originally, of course, it was closely associated with baptism, as can be clearly seen in the earlier forms of the rites of Christian initiation, for confirmation is the normal completion of baptism, and the Fathers in the primitive Church often regarded the administration of the two sacraments as one single rite.

The practice at Rome in the third century can be seen from the *Apostolic Tradition* of Hippolytus, where confirmation is administered by a collective laying-on of hands[7] during the recitation of a prayer asking for the sending of the Holy Spirit and his grace on the newly baptized, the anointing of the head of each candidate, the *consignatio*

[6] See *What is a Priest?* by Joseph Lécuyer, C.S.Sp., *passim.*
[7] It seems that it must have been done collectively since the accompanying prayer referred to the candidates in the plural.

of the forehead and the kiss of peace. The rite consisted, then, of the laying-on of hands and the anointing.

From an examination of the Sacramentaries (the Gelasian and the *Hadrianum*) it seems that the rite remained very much the same during the fifth to the eighth centuries as it had done in the time of Hippolytus, though the formula for the laying-on of hands had evolved and now made mention of the seven gifts of the Holy Spirit. The unction and *consignatio* were joined together and became an unction of the forehead in the form of a cross during which the bishop pronounced the formula *Signum Christi in vitam aeternam*. The rite concluded with the kiss of peace.

These rites formed the second portion of the combined rite of Christian initiation (that is, baptism, confirmation and communion) and it was only in the ninth century or perhaps a little earlier that confirmation came to be commonly separated from baptism. As a consequence some small additions were made to the rite in order to enhance its solemnity; an entrance chant and one for the conclusion of the rite were inserted together with a collect. At Rome (eleventh–twelfth centuries) the laying-on of hands at the beginning of the rite was done individually and it was Durandus' Pontifical which substituted the collective imposition; so it has remained in the modern rite. Durandus also in place of the former kiss of peace substituted the light blow on the cheek. The accompanying words (*pax tecum*) are all that remain of the former practice. Durandus found some authority for the substitution in French Pontificals of his own time but he could only justify it by invoking a questionable symbolical interpretation, saying that it was a sign of friendship or was a symbol of the difficulties and sufferings, perhaps even martyrdom, that the Christian will have to undergo. Benedict XIV, as we have seen, modified the anointing rite by directing that the bishop should lay his right hand on the candidate's head while signing his forehead with the cross.

The two principal formulas for the administration of the

sacrament of confirmation are the invocation at the beginning of the rite and the formula of anointing. The first mentioned, which follows the entrance chant and versicles, is said by the bishop as, in the words of the rubric, he "stretches out his hands towards those to be confirmed" (this amounts to a collective laying-on of hands):

> Almighty and everlasting God, you have been pleased to regenerate these servants of yours by water and the Holy Ghost and have given them forgiveness of all their sins; send forth upon them your sevenfold Spirit, the Holy Paraclete from heaven. Amen.
> The Spirit of wisdom and understanding. Amen.
> The Spirit of counsel and fortitude. Amen.
> The Spirit of knowledge and godliness. Amen.
> Fill them with the Spirit of your fear and sign them with the sign of the cross in mercy for eternal life, through Christ our Lord.

The other formula, that for the anointing, runs as follows:

> N., I sign you with the sign of the cross and I confirm you with the chrism of salvation, in the name of the Father, and of the Son and of the Holy Spirit.

Of these two formulas the first is the most ancient and goes back in substance to the very beginning. Indeed, in the Acts of the Apostles we read that Peter and John "prayed for them that they might receive the Holy Spirit", and just afterwards, "Then the apostles began to lay their hands on them, so that the Holy Spirit was given them" (Acts 8. 15–18). The formula of invocation is found in all the earliest liturgical documents: "the Holy Spirit," says Tertullian, "is conferred on the neophytes by prayer and the laying-on of hands." The development of the formula by the adding of mention of the gifts of the Holy Spirit occurred probably in the fourth century in connection with the reconciliation of heretics.

Until the time of St Gregory the Great the laying-on of hands with prayer was regarded as the only essential formula[8] and the Gelasian Sacramentary rubric makes it quite clear that this was so: *Ad consignandum imponit eis manum in his verbis*. Now at this time the laying-on of hands was made collectively and the signing of each candidate on the forehead was probably instituted to signify the application to each individual of the effect produced by the laying-on of hands.

The formula for the anointing is now essential since it constitutes the actual form of the sacrament but it has varied considerably from early times down to quite a late period. One of its earliest forms was that in Hippolytus: "I anoint you with holy oil in the Lord, the Father almighty and Christ Jesus and the Holy Spirit." In the Gelasian Sacramentary the formula was a simple acclamation ("The sign of Christ for eternal life") and the Gregorian Sacramentary gives no words at all. And so the different variations can be traced in the liturgical books following localities, but the present formula is to be found in the tenth century in the papal Ordinarium.[9]

The dedication of churches

This is one of the longest and most complex rites in the Pontifical. It is made up of the fusion of two principal elements, the ancient Roman ritual for the consecration of a church and the rites which were incorporated into the Roman books from sources north of the Alps. The present short description cannot do more than attempt to distinguish the two elements.

The Roman consecration ritual, which developed after the Peace of the Church under Constantine when Christians were able to restore their churches and build new ones, consisted

---

[8] Cf. St Jerome, *Altercatio Luciferiani et orthodoxi*, *P.L.* 23, 143.
[9] *Ordo Romanus X* to be found in *P.L.* 78, 1017.

essentially in the celebration of Mass. Primitively this was the sole rite of dedication. This is the notion to be found in St Cyprian and St John Chrysostom (who wrote, "The altar is holy when it has received on it the Body of Christ").

A further element was added towards the end of the fourth century with the translation to the new church of the relics of saints, a very popular ceremony which was described by St Ambrose on the occasion of the dedication of the basilica later to be known as Sant' Ambrogio Maggiore. At Rome, on the other hand, the bodies of the saints were left undisturbed until the middle of the seventh century and usually basilicas were built over the tomb of a martyr with the altar in direct contact with the body. In the sixth century the use of what have been called votive relics was introduced (*brandea*); for these the altar was constructed as a mausoleum over a tomb. The sprinkling of blessed (exorcized) water round the building mentioned by St Gregory seems to have been done only in the case of the purification of a pagan temple.

In Rome, then, the two characteristic ceremonies were the translation and burying of relics in the altar together with the celebration of Mass; in Gaul, the whole rite is dominated by the consecration of the altar with multiple unctions and other rites; the translation of the relics was effected when this was concluded, almost as an afterthought. By the time of the liturgical reform of Pepin the Short the rite has assumed further complication: the bishop knocks at the door before entering, he marks out on the floor the Greek and Latin alphabets[10]; to the mixture of wine and water (used

[10] The meaning of this strange ceremony, said to be of Celtic origin, is hard to find. It has been suggested that it is connected with the primitive marking out of boundaries before taking possession of land and that the lines of letters signify the universality of the Church in space (she contains all races, speaks all languages) and in time (she stretches from the beginning—alpha—to the end—omega); the St Andrew's cross is the first letter of Christ's name; it is he who takes possession of the building.

formerly for sprinkling the building and of Byzantine origin)
he now adds salt and ashes; unctions of altar and wall have
become more complex and numerous and the whole rite is
encompassed with the singing of psalms and anthems which
emphasize the ritual acts.

From the Romano-German Pontificals of the end of the
tenth century through the Roman Pontifical of the twelfth
century and Durandus of Mende's book these complex ceremonies have passed into the modern Roman book, though
Durandus' influence seems generally to have been in the
direction of complexity and length. There are the seven
preparatory psalms, the *Veni Creator,* the unction of the
door and numerous collects all added by him.[11]

THE ROMAN RITUAL

The Ritual is that book of the Roman rite which contains
all the services performed by a priest that are not in the
Missal or Breviary, though certain matters (like the Office
of the Dead) are also included for the sake of convenience.
The Ritual is the most recent official book of the Roman
rite and even nowadays it has not been made obligatory in
the same way that the Pontifical was or the Breviary and
Missal. In the Constitution of Paul V prefixed to the first
edition of the Roman Ritual (1614) instead of phrases such
as are to be found in previous pontifical documents regard-
ing Missal, Breviary or Pontifical (for example, *in virtute
sanctae obedientiae praecipientes,* "commanding in virtue of
holy obedience") we find the pope exhorting churchmen to
use the new Ritual (*hortamur in Domino ... ut in posterum
utantur*), and so on. Without going into the precise position
under canon law, which is hardly to our purpose in this context, it can at least be said that in practice all over Europe
local Rituals held their ground and, in France, Germany

[11] The reform of the second part of the Pontifical in 1961 has
led to a curtailment of some of the excessive length of the dedication
ceremony; it is mentioned below, p. 103.

and Austria, for instance, down to the present time, these books have remained in use. But the Roman Ritual, like the other reformed books of an earlier date, had its effect on local usages, and just as Breviaries and Missals, when the reformed Roman books were not adopted *en bloc,* were corrected and in many ways brought into line with the Roman books, so local Rituals frequently took over many of the rites and practices of the Roman Ritual. Indeed the latter seems to envisage such local variations; it provides the normal pattern to be followed everywhere and the source from which formularies wanting in national and regional Rituals are to be taken. A little earlier the Council of Trent had made it very clear that it desired (*vehementer optat*) that, in addition to what it had prescribed, the laudable rites and customs of particular provinces or countries should be retained.

Like the Pontifical, the Ritual is derived from the Sacramentaries. The Pontifical was the first book to emerge and originally it contained, as we have seen, in addition to the functions strictly reserved to a bishop, certain rites that could be performed by a priest. Baptism is a case in point. Until the time of Durandus it frequently figured in the book used by bishops. With the growth of the Church in the early centuries, as parishes were organized away from the immediate presence of the bishop, provision had to be made for the administration of the sacraments by priests; they were expected to possess a *libellus ordinis* or a *libellus officialis.* The fourth Council of Toledo (633) under St Isidore decreed that bishops must provide each priest whom they sent to a parish with a *libellus ordinis.* We do not know what exactly it contained but it has been supposed that it was a kind of Ritual.

Examination of a modern Roman Ritual reveals the fact that the book is divided into sections (*tituli*: thus *titulus II* contains everything to do with baptism, *titulus IX* is a long section on blessings of all kinds) and it is known that originally most of these sections were separate little books (*libelli*).

The *ordo baptismi* was often a little book of this kind and in larger books like the Stowe Missal or that of Bobbio, in which it is included, it was inserted in such a way that it could be easily detached. And there are references to an *ordo baptismi* as a separate *libellus*. *Titulus IV* in the modern Ritual is very short giving the bare minimum for the sacrament of penance; originally much more guidance was given to the priest in the administration of this sacrament, including a whole list of suitable penances and kinds of sins; all this was in the book known as the *Penitential*. Similarly the blessings now collected together in *titulus IX* formed the *Benedictional*.

During the Middle Ages the various booklets containing these elements were collected together in one volume containing all the occasional offices needed by a priest. The first compilations under the title of *Manuale* or *Liber manualis* were made in the eleventh–twelfth centuries for the convenience of priests in monasteries; use of these books spread to the parishes where, under various names (*Alphabeta sacerdotis, Sacerdotale, Pastorale*, etc.), they became the parish priest's indispensable guide in the administration of the sacraments and a handy manual of canon law in relation to them.

More even than the Pontifical the Ritual was subject to considerable local variation; some of this has persisted to the present day and can be seen in the local Rituals in use or the additions or appendices to the Roman Ritual allowed for some countries. In the nature of things this must be so. The rite of marriage, for example, is everywhere surrounded with a whole context of social customs and traditions and it is natural that some of them should be reflected in the liturgy. Such local variation in the Middle Ages went very far indeed and by the time of the Council of Trent, as we have seen with the other liturgical books, there was a press-

ing need for the elimination of abuses and for the achievement of a certain measure of uniformity.

The Ritual was the last book to be subject to reform.
As in the case of the Pontifical, various books were issued
in Rome with a view to obtaining uniformity but no official
sanction was given to them. Castellani in 1537 published a
Sacerdotale; in 1579 another version appeared edited by a
canon of the Lateran, Francesco Samarino; this in its turn was
revised by Angelo Rocca. In 1586 Giulio Antonio Santorio,
Cardinal of St Severina, produced another handbook for the
use of priests, basing his compilation on the editions of 1537
and 1579, which he drew up, Paul V says, "after long study
and with much industry and labour" (*longo studio, multaque
industria et labore*). This was the book which formed the
principal source for the Roman Ritual issued by Paul V in
1614.

The persistence of local Rituals has already been referred
to, but it will not be out of place here to mention the continued use in England of the Sarum Manual during penal
days (an edition of it was printed in Rouen in 1610); it
certainly was not displaced by the Roman Ritual for some
years and no doubt had the situation in the country been
normal it would have continued in use. Its successor, modelled
largely on the Roman Ritual (from which were taken the
rites for all the sacraments except matrimony), was called
Ordo administrandi sacramenta and contained a revised version of the Sarum rite for matrimony. The title page referred
indeed to ancient English customs by saying that it contained
certain additions from the old English Ritual (*nonnullis
adiectis ex antiquo rituali anglicano*). The revised recension
of the Sarum marriage service has continued in use in the
British Isles down to the present day.

Some slight revisions and additions (particularly of blessings) have been made in the course of the three centuries
or so that the Roman Ritual has been in existence, but it still
remains in essence the book that was published by Paul V
in 1614.

CHAPTER V

THE LITURGICAL REFORM
OF THE TWENTIETH
CENTURY

After the reform set on foot by the Council of Trent the books of the Roman liturgy remained in all matters save unessential details what they had become as a result of this reform. Whereas for roughly fifteen hundred years liturgy had been in a state of continual evolution (though that is not to say that all developments, particularly some that occurred in the Middle Ages, were fortunate), after Trent it entered on a period of what has been called "changeless-ness or rubricism".[1] By the end of the nineteenth century it was beginning to be seen that at least in some respects the liturgy needed reform though there seems to have been no idea that such reform was a fundamental requirement; rather was it regarded as a tidying up process to be applied to matters like the calendar.

In the first years of the twentieth century the revival of liturgical studies that had taken place in the nineteenth century began to have its effect. Many liturgical texts had been published and the work of men like Dom Guéranger, Mgr Duchesne, Mgr Batiffol, Edmund Bishop, Christopher

[1] Theodor Klauser, *The Western Liturgy and its History*, translated by F. L. Cross (London, 1952), p. 49.

Wordsworth, Möhler, together with the long-term effects of the Oxford Movement, were all instrumental in bringing to the fore a less restricted view of liturgy. The need for reform of the liturgy was gradually realized and was mentioned in some quarters[2] though in general the liturgy was so misunderstood that need for its reform was not perceived.

ST PIUS X'S REFORM

Leo XIII set up an historical commission of the Congregation of Rites but it does not seem to have accomplished anything during his pontificate or in the years immediately following; in fact it is only recently that its work has begun to bear fruit. It was left to St Pius X to initiate the desired reform; he did so by his Bull, *Divino afflatu* which was issued in 1911; its prescriptions came into force on January 1st, 1913. Yet it requires to be pointed out that this reform was preceded by another which, though it was in connection with the liturgy, affected not only the clergy but principally the congregations committed to their charge. At the beginning of St Pius X's pontificate it is true to say that liturgy was regarded as something to do with the interpretation of rubrics rather than as the worship of the whole Christian body and it was commonly seen as the special concern of the clergy or even as a monastic speciality or, on a last analysis, as the preserve of certain eccentrics among the better-educated clergy or laity. A new emphasis, amounting to a revolution, was effected in the early years of this century by St Pius X, though perhaps it is only now, after upwards of half a century, that the practical implications of his great achievement are beginning to be realized.

It has been necessary to point this out because in writing of the history of the liturgical books in however brief a

[2] For instance by Mgr Batiffol at the end of his *History of the Breviary* (in the first edition of 1893, that is; when the last was published in 1912 much of what he had asked for had been granted).

form it is difficult not to give the impression that all the technical questions raised are hardly ones that affect the congregation in church; in reality they affect them very closely. To put the matter quite shortly, it was the two reforms at the beginning of St Pius X's pontificate, reforms of a pastoral nature, that led to the rubrical reform of 1911. The one created the climate for the other.

St Pius X saw clearly the dangers of artificiality, of lifelessness, of ritualism, and by his *Motu proprio* (1903) on sacred music and by the decree on frequent communion restored to the faithful the two great means of their taking their proper part in the worship of the Church. If there had been any doubt before, there could be none after these important acts— the liturgy could no longer be viewed as the special preserve of the monasteries or of an intellectual *élite*: St Pius X, in measured words, called active participation in the holy mysteries "the foremost and indispensable fount" of the true Christian spirit. "Filled as we are," he writes

> with a most ardent desire to see the true Christian spirit flourish in every respect and be preserved by all the faithful, we deem it necessary to provide before aught else for the sanctity and dignity of the temple in which the faithful assemble for no other object than that of acquiring this spirit from its foremost and indispensable fount which is the active participation in the most holy mysteries and in the solemn and public prayer of the Church.

Of the end there can be no argument; St Pius X has clearly defined the means by which it is to be attained. As we look back over the past half century we can see that it was St Pius X who inaugurated the movement of the faithful back to the liturgy though perhaps it is only today that we are beginning to feel the effects of this movement.

St Pius X's liturgical reform decreed by the Bull *Divino afflatu* affected chiefly the Breviary but by reason of its changes in the calendar of the Breviary influenced the Missal as well. The purpose of the reform was twofold. Firstly, it was intended to bring the liturgical year into greater prominence by allowing the more frequent celebration of the ferial and Sunday Offices and Masses, secondly, by a rearrangement of the Psalter in the Breviary (referred to below) the Office was made slightly shorter, especially on Sundays. The chief points of the reform as it affected the Missal were to do with the calendar; no great deletions were made from it save for the feasts fixed on certain Sundays (those on the Sundays in October, for example, or after Easter) but by making the rule that no feast of lesser rank than a double of the second class could be celebrated on Sunday, or transferred if its celebration was impeded, the majority of Sundays were at once restored to normal celebration in the churches of the world. By making the Sunday Office of more manageable length—it became slightly shorter than the normal saint's Office—the clergy were led to abandon their desire for a shorter saint's Office on a Sunday. Thus quite simply, by an easy alteration in the rubrics governing the calendar, an abuse that had been apparent for many centuries past, and which St Pius V's reform did little to check, was swept away by St Pius X.

The state of affairs prevailing before 1911 both in the general calendar of the Breviary and the special calendars belonging to dioceses and religious Orders can only be described as anarchic. No sooner had St Pius V reduced the feasts of saints to numbers of reasonable proportion in relation to the Offices of the season than the inverse process began all over again and by 1910 the ferial and Sunday Office and Mass had practically disappeared; inspection of some of the calendars of those days shows that save for the Sundays of Advent and Lent, Ash Wednesday and Holy Week, together with the great festivals like Easter and Whitsun, the ferial and Sunday Office for the rest of the year was not celebrated at all.

One of the reasons for the dislike of the Sunday Office was its great length. Matins of three nocturns contained eighteen complete psalms, Prime was long (it included Ps. 117 and the Athanasian Creed), and this long Office occurred on the day on which the clergy were most occupied. St Pius V's attempt to reform the Breviary had to some extent been a reaction against the Breviary of Quignonez; the old Roman distribution of the psalms (abandoned by Quignonez) was retained. St Pius X saw that a new distribution of the psalms was the only way to remedy the situation; to those who regretted the passing of the old scheme for the distribution of the Psalter the reply was easy: it had already been abolished in practice, since on very few days of the year was it ever used and never were the 150 psalms recited in the course of a week.

To ensure that the complete Psalter was said in the course of a week, and without adding to the length of the Office, the psalms were distributed over the days of the week with variable psalms for each day at every hour. Hitherto at Matins, Lauds and Vespers the psalms varied but at the other Hours they were invariable. A further rubric, by directing that the ordinary feasts of saints should be celebrated with the ferial psalmody and with the lessons of the first nocturn from the Scripture lessons in the proper of the season, ensured that the Psalter was usually recited in the week and that the course of Scripture was read on most days of the year. It is noteworthy that St Pius X's reform of the Breviary adopted certain of the principles first advocated by the eighteenth-century French Breviaries—division of the longer psalms, use of variable psalms at all Hours etc.

St Pius X said that his reform was the first stage for the reform of Missal and Breviary (*primum gradum ad Romani Breviarii et Missalis emendationem*)[3]; he intended to reform the calendar and restore it to its primitive state (that is, with far fewer feasts), to correct the lectionary and ensure a better choice and distribution of the matter in the Breviary.

[3] Motu proprio *Abhinc duos annos*, October 23rd, 1913.

The work to be done was summed up by Mgr Piacenza[4] as follows:

1. Principles were to be established according to which feasts were admitted into the general calendar of the Roman rite and their degree of importance determined.
2. The hagiographical lessons (i.e. of the second nocturn) to be revised according to the principles of sound historical criticism.
3. Apocryphal lessons from the Fathers to be eliminated.
4. A general revision of the rubrics.

The time was hardly ripe for such a thoroughgoing reform and nothing was done for the time being. Other preoccupations were to the fore during the pontificates of Benedict XV and Pius XI, though the fact that men's minds were hardly prepared for further reform can be discerned from the fact that during the next twenty-five years a number of unnecessary feasts were again added to the calendar.

PIUS XII'S REFORM

One result of the Second World War was the emergence of a new approach to liturgy. Times of stress had provoked a searching reappraisal of the position of the Church in the modern world and in addition the mentality of those who had been constrained to worship in prison camps or on the battle field, under aerial bombardment or in other perilous conditions, was affected very strongly by these factors. It turned their thoughts to essentials. The new generation both of clergy and layfolk was inspired principally by a desire for authenticity. Fr Yves M. J. Congar has summed it up very clearly. People, he said, had come to desire

> authentic actions which really correspond with what they claim
> to signify. Sincerity has always been a requirement of the

[4] P. Piacenza, *In constitutionem Divino afflatu SS. D.N. Pii papae X ... commentarium,* Rome, 1912.

Christian character, but in modern man there is an irrepressible need of sincerity, especially in matters of worship and in his relations with God. He wants an altar that is an altar and not a stand for flowers and statues; an Easter... vigil that is a vigil and not a morning service hastily gone through; a Mass that is really the praise and sacrifice of a community one in faith, and not a mere rite, taking place for its own sake before the congregation, whether they follow it or not. That is the point: there are too many things with us which have become "rites", that is "things" with an existence of their own, complete; the "directions for use", necessary for validity, must be observed without troubling whether they are the acts of a *person*. As Abbé Michonneau has rightly observed, men do not live by rites and our parishes are un-attractive because our "Christianity appears as a ritualism which changes nothing in the life of those who practise it". In our wonderful and holy Catholic liturgy, as it is often per-formed, there are too many things whose original meaning is no longer really honoured and which have been reduced to the state of an atrophied organ, ritualized vestiges of an action which originally was the real deed of a man or a living community.[5]

It was amid this ferment of ideas thrown up by the Second World War that the second stage of the liturgical reform set on foot by St Pius X was continued by Pius XII. It pro-ceeded by stages, though fairly quickly, after the end of the war.

New Latin translation of the Psalms

Pius XII commissioned the Jesuits of the Biblical Institute in Rome to make a new translation of the Psalter, more in conformity with the Hebrew text and bringing out its mean-ing more clearly. The version in official use in the Church ever since the adoption of the Breviary of the Curia in the thirteenth century was that known as the Gallican Psalter, the second of St Jerome's revisions of the Latin translation

[5] *Vraie et fausse réforme dans l'Église* (Paris, 1952), p. 50.

of the psalms. In Italy however it did not displace the old Roman Psalter (which still survives at St Peter's, Rome) until the publication of the Breviary of St Pius V. In many ways the Gallican version is unsatisfactory, there are a multitude of Hebraisms and literal translations of a corrupt text which in places do not make sense. Nevertheless, in its favour it can be said that it has become so traditional in the Church, that its phraseology has become so closely integrated with the liturgy that to change it for something very different was a step of great importance. The new version was not entirely successful; although in many instances it made the psalms more intelligible, in many others, with no gain in clarity, changes were made which upset the rhythm of the psalm verse for no obvious reason. The new version was welcomed almost universally; the decree (*In cotidianis precibus*) of March 24th, 1945, authorized its optional use in the Roman rite, though at first it seemed as if what happened with Urban VIII's revised hymns was about to occur over again with the new version of the Psalter: publishers of Breviaries at once began to print the new version exclusively, new Masses added to the Missal had the new version in the chanted portions and as new editions of the other liturgical books appeared they too contained the new psalms. It looked as if the new version would be made obligatory very shortly. In the event this did not happen, and gradually the climate of opinion began to change. The new version proved not entirely satisfactory for public singing of the psalms and many who at first adopted it reverted to the traditional version. The fact that it was not adopted by the Benedictines, the one section in the Church that has remained particularly faithful to the public celebration of the Office, is not without significance.

It has come to be seen, in fact, that while the Gallican Psalter needs correction in certain places this could be done while preserving its traditional rhythm and vocabulary.

The simplification of the rubrics

On March 23rd, 1955, the Congregation of Rites issued a decree entitled *De rubricis ad simpliciorem formam reductis* which continued the rubrical reform set on foot by St Pius X. Its principal provisions showed once again that reform of the liturgy could be largely achieved by careful regulation of the calendar. It was quite clearly an interim reform and it seemed clear also that further steps in the same direction were to be taken.

The *Pater, Ave* and *Credo* at the beginning of the Hours were suppressed, together with the anthem of our Lady at the end (except for the anthem at the end of the Compline), the shorter *Preces* (known as *Preces dominicales*) at Prime and Compline were also abolished, as well as the suffrage of the saints at Lauds and Vespers; the Athanasian Creed was no longer to be said at Prime on Sundays except on the feast of the Blessed Trinity.[6] First Vespers (that is, on the evening before) was in future only to be said for Sundays and first-class or second-class feasts. The rite of semidouble was abolished together with most vigils and many octaves—only the octaves of Christmas, Easter and Whitsun were retained.

The chief merit of this reform of the rubrics was that it abolished certain complicated additions to the Office and at the same time did something to lighten it. The abolition of the semidouble Office meant, also, the disappearance of an anomaly. Originally a double feast (there were perhaps half a dozen in the year) meant, it appears, a feast with an octave which was celebrated on the eighth day (and not during the intervening days—Easter and Whitsun excepted of course). In addition, such feasts were holidays of obligation. When it was desired to establish a feast day of some importance, but without an octave or making it a holiday, the idea of a semidouble was adopted. It became in fact

[6] This restriction in the use of the Athanasian Creed had already been laid down in the Benedictine Breviary of 1915.

a ritual prescription affecting principally the clergy; since by the time of the 1955 reform the rite of double had also become very common, the *raison d'être* for the celebration of a feast as a semidouble no longer remained. Much the same might be said of octaves, for most of them (those known heretofore as common octaves) were frequently reduced to an extra collect at Mass or commemoration at Lauds and Vespers. Some surprise was expressed that the octave of the Epiphany should have shared the same fate as the others, but it does not appear that this octave is of early origin. As late as the twelfth century the Epiphany was a semi-double feast.

Next in chronological order came the reform of the Holy Week services (by the decree *Maxima Redemptionis nostrae mysteria* of November 16th, 1955), but it will be more convenient to speak first of the continuation of the reform of Breviary and Missal by the *motu proprio* of July 25th, 1960, for though it was signed by the present pope, John XXIII, the work was initiated under his predecessor, Pius XII. The *motu proprio* (*Rubricarum instructum*) was accompanied by a general decree of the Congregation of Rites promulgating a new code of rubrics for Missal and Breviary.

Very largely this reform consisted in the codification of the previous reforms in the Breviary and Missal; some new elements, however, were added. The codification of the rubrics and their entire redrafting was long overdue; the interim reform of 1955 made the provision of new rubrics a matter of some urgency.

Before publication of the new editions of the liturgical books consequent on the reform of 1906 the Breviary and Missal began with the rubrics of the typical editions of 1900 (in the case of the Breviary) and 1901 (for the Missal) which, with some slight modifications, reproduced those of the seventeenth-century reform under St Pius V. For well nigh half a century these rubrics had been almost entirely out of date and required to be supplemented for the most part by the

Variationes et additiones (printed immediately afterwards) bringing them into agreement with St Pius X's reform.

The principal simplification of the rubrics was attained by a new classification of feasts into three classes—the old scheme was entirely swept away. The engaging simplicity of the opening sentence of the old rubrics ("The daily Office is double, semidouble or simple") was belied in practice; there were five classes of double, for instance, and even this did not exhaust the variety of distinctions between feasts. The various categories of doubles were divided into primary and secondary (the feast of the Sacred Heart was a primary double of the first class, that of the Precious Blood a secondary double of the first class) and, if these were inadequate, there were further distinctions on which to fall back to decide which feast should obtain precedence on a particular day. But the classification of feasts in the Roman Breviary was simplicity itself compared to the many complexities of the medieval Breviaries: in addition to *duplex, semiduplex* and *simplex* there were feasts *novem lectionum, celebre, solemne* and in some places *totum duplex* and even *triplex.* (Until recently the modern Premonstratensian Breviary kept most of these categories.)

The new classification of feasts into three classes therefore was a considerable simplification. Its general effect on the calendar can be explained by saying (though this is an approximation) that first-class feasts are those that previously were doubles of the first class, second-class feasts those that were doubles of the second class and third-class feasts those that were greater doubles, doubles or simples. The most far-reaching consequence of this classification is that third-class feasts are equivalent in practice to simples in the old classification and that all Sundays take precedence over most second-class feasts.

Despite its importance the Sunday Office has nevertheless been reduced in length. Matins now consists of nine psalms and three lessons, the first two made up of the Scripture lessons formerly appointed for the first nocturn, the third the former seventh lesson of the homily on the Gospel. On the third-class feasts the lessons are made up of the first two from the course of Scripture, the third from the former legend of the saint (the contracted form is used). We saw in the history of the Breviary during the Middle Ages how the lectionary was abbreviated. The further abbreviation that has resulted as a consequence of the latest reform reduces the lessons in the Breviary to merely token form. An example is furnished by the third lesson for the fourth Sunday after the Epiphany. The lesson is an excerpt from St Jerome's homily on the Gospel of the day; it runs as follows:

> The fifth sign was that which he did when going into the ship from Capharnaum he commanded the winds and the sea. The sixth when in the country of the Gerasenes he gave the devils power over the swine. The seventh when he entered his city and cured the second paralysed man in his bed. For the first paralysed man to be cured was the centurion's servant.

That is all of the homily that is read. It seems obvious that a further stage in the reform now in progress will be a revision of the lectionary of the Breviary. (The matter is referred to below.)

Certain feasts were reduced in rank or simply deleted from the calendar. Thus our Lady of Mount Carmel, our Lady of Ransom, and the feast of the Stigmata of St Francis are now merely commemorations, though no doubt these feasts retain their respective rank in the calendars of the Carmelites, Mercedarians and Franciscans, being thus, as is fitting, domestic celebrations in the religious Orders concerned. But it is pure gain that legends like that of our Lady of Mount Carmel (July 16th) should no longer figure in the Breviary. The other feasts that are deleted from the calendar are mostly those which are duplications of one sort and another or whose history does not bear investigation.

The general effect of this reform of the calendar, therefore,

is one of considerable simplification by the removal of anomalies. The liturgy of the season now emerges more clearly
than it did before and the complications of the classifications
of feasts and ferias have been very much reduced. The
keeping of Lent with its daily Office and Mass (save for
four feast days at the most) is obviously a great gain. Look-
ing back over the past five hundred years it is clear that
we now enjoy a calendar that is a great improvement on
anything in force during that period. That for centuries the
Church's year was turned upside down with an almost daily
festival liturgy during seasons of penance seems, at first sight,
almost past belief. In reality it was merely an indication of
the difference between the true liturgical spirit and the
ritualism that passed for liturgy.

The calendar that came into force in 1961, then, is far
simpler than anything that has been known for centuries. The
length of the Office also has been reduced almost to what
Quignonez made of it, though the present Office is on traditional lines. A further much needed reform has been
effected by the insistence that the "Hours" of prayer are
meant to correspond with the times of day to which they
refer, that, for example, Compline is meant to be night
prayers said before retiring for the night and that Lauds is
the praise and prayer of the early morning. Until quite recently the timetable of choir Office in many place, and
even among religious Orders, made nonsense of the whole
conception of the Breviary as prayers for the sanctification
of hours of the day; thus Lauds was often anticipated on
the evening or afternoon of the previous day, Vespers and
Compline were habitually said in many places immediately
after the midday meal, and so on. In some of the great Roman
basilicas, the Lateran or St Peter's, for example, the whole
day's Office was said straight through from Matins to Compline at one morning session in choir. Cause for regret that
the choral Office, in use in those churches for many centuries, was given up soon after the Second World War can

be tempered by the fact that it had become a vestigial ritual largely evacuated of meaning.

With the code of canon law (1917) we reach the last stage in the evolution of the Office as a private, as distinct from a public obligation. Canon 135 is the definitive and formal law that sanctions a custom that for many years past had force of law. Clergymen in sacred orders and religious of both sexes who are under solemn vows are bound to the recitation of the Breviary Office so that to all intents and purposes it has become a clerical prayer; colour is often lent to this notion by reference to the Breviary as the "priest's prayerbook". But the history of the Office shows clearly enough that it is the prayer of the whole Church compiled for public celebration, though this hardly ever takes place in most cathedrals let alone parish churches. Here, then, under modern conditions, there is a great gap in the public worship of the Church, for the Office even in its present simplified form is hardly suitable for parochial celebration, and yet to banish the singing of psalms and the reading of the Scriptures from congregational worship seems a break with earliest tradition hard to justify. It is true that there are Scripture readings and extracts from the psalms in the first part of Mass but that is hardly sufficient. Further reform of the Breviary will have to take this aspect of the question into consideration.

Finally, reform of the lectionary appears to be urgently necessary. The present Breviary, for the Scripture lessons and the patristic extracts, is, as we have seen, an abbreviation of a *cursus* that was itself an abbreviation of a former much longer and well-balanced scheme drawn up for a different purpose: that is, it was largely monastic in origin and was intended to be read out in church. There remain too many anomalies in the calendar even in its present simplified state and there are still names commemorated in the liturgy of the Church whose continued presence it is hard to justify. Until a thorough revision of the Martyrology takes place—

and the present reform has left it untouched—proper adjustment of the calendar will be very difficult.

The new code of rubrics left the Mass practically unaltered[7] but the changes in the calendar consequent on the new rules for precedence of feasts have served to emphasize still further the seasonal liturgy. Here again further reform will have to take into account the changed conditions of the modern world.

If the new code of rubrics effected little change in the Missal the changes in the Holy Week services which were published some five years previously amounted to a major reform. The restored Easter vigil first appeared in 1951 as an experiment; it met with such widespread approval that it was soon made obligatory and the first reaction on the part of those who welcomed this reform was a desire for a similar restoration of the other Holy Week services. In fact, preparations for this were even then going on in Rome and by 1953 the texts of the reformed Maundy Thursday and Good Friday services were ready for publication, but for a variety of reasons could not then be issued.

The *Ordo Hebdomadae Sanctae,* later incorporated into the Missal, changed the whole pattern of the Holy Week liturgy. It is worthwhile noticing, too, that though, as the decree making these changes obligatory pointed out, they were made for pastoral reasons, in effect they were a return to primitive practice. The first impression produced, indeed, by examination of the new rubrics and rites was one of surprise that for so long so many anomalies could have been tolerated. The fact was, of course, that for most of the faithful general incomprehension of the rites that were performed made them very largely ritual gestures devoid of meaning. In addition, double and even threefold symbolism

---

[7] The omission of the prayers at the foot of the altar, the last Gospel or the blessing on certain occasions, and the direction that the celebrant at a high Mass is no longer to recite the Epistle and Gospel when they are sung by others, are practically the only changes in the rubrics of the *ordo Missae.*

required lengthy explanation to be made at all intelligible, the services were held at times when many could not be present so that it was small wonder that the majority of the faithful preferred the merely ancillary elements of liturgy, making more, for example, of the altar of repose on Maundy Thursday than of the Mass.

The need for reform arose from certain causes which have been at work for several centuries now. First and foremost there was the ever increasing ritualization of worship, creating a great gulf between clergy and laity in church. Then, since the early Middle Ages, the liturgical celebration of the *Triduum sacrum* had gradually been displaced from the evening to the morning, until the position was reached that what belonged to the evening or the night (Maundy Thursday Mass, Easter vigil) had been transferred to the morning and what belonged to the morning was anticipated on the previous evening or afternoon (Matins and Lauds: with the added anomaly of the candles being extinguished as darkness increased—and so a false symbolism, as so often, was invented to explain what had become a meaningless piece of ceremonial).

It will be unnecessary here to go into details of the changes effected, but two points may be made in this connection which are of paramount importance in the whole context of this reform. The first is the overriding preoccupation in the reformed Holy Week liturgy with authenticity, that authenticity which Fr Congar called for in the extract quoted above. An example will make this clear.

The whole emphasis of the restored Palm Sunday rite is on the procession. The former Palm Sunday celebration consisted of a long blessing of palms after which a "token" procession was held of clergy and choir throughout the church, with the people remaining in their places. But a procession is in reality a movement of the whole congregation in church from one point to another in order to do something; it is not a parade of ecclesiastics before an immobile congregation. In addition, the Palm Sunday procession is the typical liturgical procession: it is a re-enactment of our Lord's entry into Jerusalem in order to acclaim him and if the celebrant acts, as always, *in persona Christi*, some participation of the crowd is essential. At the beginning of Holy Week the whole Church sets out for Jerusalem to celebrate the paschal mystery.

All this is very clear from the account that has come down to us (in the *Peregrinatio Egeriae*) of what was done in Jerusalem in the fourth or fifth century. Bishops, clergy and faithful went up to Mount Olivet:

> As the eleventh hour drew near the passage from the Gospel [relating to the first procession of palms] is read. And the bishop rises and with him all the people and they set off from the top of Mount Olivet. All the people walk before the bishop singing hymns and anthems with the refrain "Blessed is he who comes in the name of the Lord". All the little children, even those who cannot walk and are carried by their parents, hold branches of palms or olive... and so the bishop is escorted as our Lord was on that day. From the top of the mount down to the city and thence to the Anastasis, going through the whole city, everyone is on foot, even the women, even persons of importance, all escort the bishop singing the anthem; and so the journey is made going quite slowly in order not to tire the crowd and it is already evening when the Anastasis is reached.

The second concern in the revised Holy Week liturgy is for the participation of the people by voice and action. The general decree bringing these changes into operation tells us that the liturgy of Holy Week possesses a special sacramental efficacy to sustain Christian life (*sacrosanctae hebdomadae liturgicae ritus... peculiari sacramentali vi et efficacia pollent ad christianam vitam alendam*). The idea that the people's active participation in the services of the Church is of importance to their lives as Christians has met, it must be confessed, with only guarded acceptance, and sometimes with outright opposition both in England and the United States: it can hardly be said to be a popular idea among Catholics in the English-speaking world. But right through the restored Holy Week services, from the direction, continually repeated, that the people are to answer *Amen* to the prayers, to the restoration of the communion on Good Friday[8] the emphasis is on complete and active participation by the faithful. Inherent in the decree is the idea that for the liturgy of Holy Week to be effective in the souls of the faithful it must be celebrated not only for them but by them. The institution of the Eucharist, the passion and death of our Lord, his resurrection on Easter night are to be celebrated, not as mysteries of the past that are merely commemorated, but as events in the yearly life of the Church and of every Christian soul. "This is the night," sings the Church at Easter, "which *today* throughout the whole world restores to grace and unites in holiness those that believe in Christ."

The Pontifical

The revision of the Pontifical was begun under Pius XII but nothing was published during his reign. He did however issue an important decree about the form and matter of

---

[8] The so-called Mass of the Presanctified on Good Friday was one of the greatest anomalies of the liturgical year. The blessed Sacrament was brought back in procession to the high altar and there then took place a rite which defied explanation. It was not Mass, yet the celebrant asked the prayers of those present for *meum ac vestrum sacrificium* and said the prayer *In spiritu humilitatis* of the offertory of the Mass. The rites with the chalice, too, were misleading. All this led up to the communion of the celebrant alone and was something of an anti-climax after what had gone before. The presence of the congregation at this part of the service seemed purposeless. The revisors were faced with the alternative either of abolishing the communion on Good Friday, and at the same time of course the reservation and altar of repose on Maundy Thursday (this would have been a return to the most primitive practice) or else of retaining the altar of repose and restoring it to its original purpose, namely reservation of the Eucharist for the communion of the faithful. They chose the latter.

ordinations that settled a controversy of some centuries standing. This was the constitution *Sacramentum ordinis* (November 30th, 1947) which laid down that the essential rite in the ordination of bishops, priests and deacons is the laying-on of hands with the corresponding formula for each order.[9] During the pontificate of the present Pope the latest result of the labours of the historical section of the Congregation of Rites has been issued; it is the revised second part of the Pontifical (*editio typica emendata*) and the first major revision of a part of the Pontifical since the time of its first issue by Clement VIII. The second part of the book concerns, it will be remembered, the blessing or consecration of things and thus it contains the consecration of a church— a long and complex rite with much ceremonial that had largely ceased to fulfil the function for which it was originally intended.

It is chiefly this rite, together with other longer blessings, that has been revised. The underlying principle of the change is a concern to abbreviate the longer rites, the modification of the text of the prayers to restore them to their earlier form where manuscript warranty for this exists, and a concern once more for participation by the people. Many of the repetitions have been deleted: thus the bishop goes round the walls of the church sprinkling them with holy water once only; the anointing of the altar and the preparation of the sepulchre for the relics is much simplified; the Greek and Latin alphabets marked out on the floor of the church are now to be before the sanctuary and only about three yards long. Throughout the rite the emphasis is laid on congregational participation, even to the extent of allowing a more popular chant or hymn to be substituted at some parts of the rite.

More than any other book of the Roman rite the Pontifical reveals both its medieval origin and the date of its definitive emergence as an obligatory liturgical book in the

[9] See in this series J. Lécuyer, C.S.Sp., *What is a Priest?* pp. 47–8.

sixteenth century. Careful examination of it shows that it is redolent both of the feudal system and of the late Renaissance. It is no surprise to find, therefore, in the revision of part II, that the blessing and imposition of the crusader's cross (*de benedictione et impositione crucis proficiscentibus in subsidium et defensionem Fidei Christianae seu recuperationem terrae sanctae*), blessings of arms and armour, the blessing of a sword and the blessing of a flag for war (*de benedictione et traditione vexilli bellici*) have now been omitted. No doubt in the revision of parts I and III other dead wood will be cut away; there seems little need to reprint in succeeding editions the order for the processional reception of the Holy Roman Emperor or the archaic questions set down (with the answers) which were formerly asked of bishops on the eve of their consecration. In addition to matter of detail like this reforms of other matters of substance are needed together with a revision of many of the purely ceremonial prescriptions.[10]

The Ritual

There has been no reform of the Roman Ritual in the same way that the Breviary and the Missal have been reformed, nor have there been changes commensurate with those of the second part of the Pontifical. On the other hand, there have been many changes allowed for local use either by the permission for the use of partial translations of the Roman Ritual (bilingual Rituals) or by the approval of reformed local Rituals (often in the shape of an appendix to the Roman Ritual: thus the German Ritual is called *Collectio Rituum ad instar appendicis Ritualis Romani*). It was pointed out above that the Roman Ritual has never been made obligatory in the same way that the other books have and it will be remembered, also, that the Council of Trent expressed itself as desiring (*vehementer optat*) that

[10] See below, in the Appendix, p. 109, what is said of the *Ceremoniale Episcoporum*.

in addition to what it had prescribed the laudable rites and customs of particular provinces or countries should be retained. There is no doubt, therefore, that the Ritual forms a somewhat special case among the liturgical books and that because local variations have been permitted for centuries past the introduction of some vernacular into the administration of the sacraments and other rites has been attained more easily as a consequence. In any case, a small amount of vernacular has always been necessary; the interrogations in baptism, the expression of consent in marriage, have of necessity to be made in the mother tongue. It is a small step to add to this the translation of some of the prayers or blessings preceding or following these parts of the rites.

The list of concessions in this matter is impressive[11] and generally speaking Rome has made no difficulties about granting reasonable requests; indeed in some cases bishops have been urged to propose bilingual Rituals for approval.

Not all the local Rituals approved contain the same amount of vernacular. In some places (Germany, Belgium, the United States, Ireland) the opportunity has been taken to reform some of the rites; in France and those countries whose Rituals were approved on the pattern of the French *Rituale parvum* no changes were made in the rites and the amount of vernacular allowed was smaller.

Translation of some of the prayers of the Ritual has revealed the importance of careful study of the history of the rites that the book contains[12] as well as the need in many cases for revision of some of the rites themselves. The need for adaptation has been felt particularly in the mission field

[11] Bilingual Rituals have been authorized for Poland (1927), Yugoslavia (1930), Austria (1935), France (1947), Germany (1950), Spain (1950), Italy (1953), U.S.A. (1954), England and Wales (1959) and Ireland (1959).

[12] Thus the English and Irish Rituals both contain certain errors of translation in the baptism rite; the French Ritual too contained similar errors—some of these were corrected in a subsequent edition.

where rites, which in non-essentials achieved their definitive form in sixteenth-century Italy, are not always suitable for use, say, in Borneo or Australia. The whole question of the revision of the Ritual was considered at length in an important paper of a symposium held at Nijmegen[13] a few years ago. There Mgr Lino Gonzaga y Rasdesales outlined various *desiderata* in the matter of adaptation which are too detailed to be considered here, but one of his conclusions is certainly relevant to the present chapter on liturgical reform:

> Active participation requires first of all understanding of the action participated in. Without this understanding, the participants will turn into automatons. Cardinal Goma said, "To separate the idea from the action and to reduce Christian life to the automatism of some ritualistic practices which cannot be understood are to mutilate the action, cutting the joint through which it receives the sap; it is making religion a somatic function" (p. 196).

By means of the vernacular Rituals it can be said that almost everywhere a measure of useful reform of the Roman Ritual has been achieved. Nevertheless, it is the Roman Ritual which is intended to be the norm for the local Rituals; it is clear therefore that, apart from the adaptation to different parts of the world that will be ultimately necessary, there are many points needing reform; taken singly they might seem unimportant details but cumulatively they amount to very much more.

Thus the restoration and a certain refashioning of the rite of baptism is an obvious case. Even in missionary countries, where there is an organized catechumenate, there are certain anomalies, but in countries like England or the U.S.A. in practice the instruction of an unbaptized convert is in fact a catechumenate, though the rites belonging to it are telescoped together at a ceremony drawn up for the

[13] *Liturgy and the Missions: The Nijmegen Papers,* edited by Johannes Hofinger, S.J.

baptism of infants. Whether in Latin or in English what is done seems calculated to evacuate significant rites of their meaning.[14] Nor does there seem any reason for keeping *Ego conjungo vos* (it has already been deleted from the German Ritual) in the marriage service, particularly as the Ritual makes it clear that the priest may use other words to declare that the couple are now man and wife. The formula *Ego conjungo* is the lingering relic of an out-of-date theological position no longer held now by anyone. A funeral in the Roman rite is a jejune service consisting principally of the procession to the grave. Here again, pastoral reasons would seem to call for a better and more intelligible rite, perhaps wholly in the vernacular, with some emphasis on an integral Christian view of death.[15]

With the great movements that are at work in the Church today, the liturgical movement, the biblical movement, the renewal of theology, in questions of worship particularly we are emerging from the nineteenth-century outlook that has too long prevailed. Then the worship of the Church was remote from the culture and devotion of the faithful so that they were obliged to take refuge in private devotions of all sorts which proliferated to such an extent that in the popular image of the Church these practices were taken more often than not as the fundamentals of Catholicism. The purpose of liturgical reform, at whatever period it takes place, is to make the Church's worship more nearly the living worship of all the faithful and it is at periods of decadence like the

[14] As this book goes to press news comes that the Congregation of Rites has allowed the rite of baptism of adults to be performed in seven distinct steps, spaced out according to progress made in catechetical instruction. And most of the rite is allowed to be in the vernacular. It will now have to be translated and added to the English Ritual since hitherto in the British Isles the rite of infant baptism has anomalously been used for adults also.

[15] The traditional psalm, before 1614, at a funeral was Ps. 113 (*In exitu Israel*), the Easter psalm and one full of significance for a funeral; the substitution of Ps. 50 (*Miserere*) betrays the compiler's preoccupations.

nineteenth century that the faithful are led to adopt other means of giving expression to their religious needs. At the present time the reform of the liturgical books of the Roman rite still continues and it is likely that before many more years are past we shall see far more striking changes, never of course in essentials, but in many of the elements that no longer fulfil the function for which they were intended.

SUBSIDIARY BOOKS OF THE ROMAN RITE

In addition to the principal books of the Roman rite described in the foregoing chapters the subsidiary books are here included for the sake of completeness; they consist of books giving ceremonial instructions, books providing the chant for the various Offices and Mass, and books which are extracts from Missal, Breviary or Pontifical and are published apart for the sake of convenience.

1. The *Ceremoniale Episcoporum* was published by order of Clement VIII (Brief *Cum novissime,* July 14th, 1600); the latest typical edition is that which appeared under Leo XIII (1886). The sources of this book, which might be called the last of the *Ordines Romani,* are to be found in the *Ceremoniale sanctae romanae Ecclesiae* (1516). Parts of the book are now out of date by reason of the changes in the Pontifical and the introduction of the new Holy Week services.

More even than the Pontifical the *Ceremoniale* reflects a different age of liturgical development. It is providing the code for worship in cathedrals and collegiate churches and so it takes for granted the daily singing of the Office in choir. One wonders what its compilers would have thought of the abandonment of the daily choral Office at the Lateran and St Peter's where it had been in use for something like fifteen centuries. On the other hand the *Ceremoniale* stands in need of revision. In addition to the changes in it that will have to be made as a consequence of the new rubrics of Breviary and Missal and the reformed Holy Week services it is probable that a considerable simplification of pontifical ceremonies will be effected.

2. *Memoriale rituum pro aliquibus praestantioribus sacris functionibus persolvendis in minoribus ecclesiis.* This directory for certain ceremonies for the use of small churches (Candlemas, Ash Wednesday, Holy Week, etc.) was first published by order of Benedict XIII in 1725 and the latest typical edition is that of Benedict XV (1920). The book is now largely out of date, only *tituli I* and *II* being still in force.

3. Chant books. It will be unnecessary to list them all here. The two principal books are the *Graduale Romanum* (1907) and the *Antiphonale sacrosanctae Romanae Ecclesiae pro diurnis horis* (that is, for all the Hours of the Office except Matins). The latest typical edition of the latter is that of 1919. The book needs revision to bring it into line with the changes introduced in the Office since that date. It is some commentary on the present state of affairs to notice that for upwards of half a century (since the new distribution of the Psalter in the Roman Breviary) no provision has been made for the singing of Matins.

4. *Ordo hebdomadae sanctae instauratus* (1955). The book containing the new rites for Holy Week described in Chapter V.

5. *Ritus simplex ordinis hebdomadae sanctae instaurati* (1957). Directions for the simple rite in Holy Week and taking the place of part of *Memoriale rituum.*

6. *Ritus pontificalis ordinis hebdomadae sanctae instaurati* (1957). The pontifical rite for Holy Week, replacing part of the Pontifical and of the *Ceremoniale Episcoporum.*

SELECT BIBLIOGRAPHY

In this series: AMIOT, F.: *History of the Mass*; DENIS-BOULET, Noële M.: *The Christian Calendar*; LÉCUYER, Joseph, C.S.Sp.: *What is a Priest?*; SHEPPARD, Lancelot, C.: *The Mass in the West*.

ATCHLEY, E. G. C. F. (Editor): *Ordo Romanus Primus*, London, Moring, 1905.

BATIFFOL, Pierre: *History of the Roman Breviary*, London and New York, Longmans, 1912.

BEDE, The Venerable: *The Ecclesiastical History of the English People*, translated by Thomas Stapleton, London, Burns and Oates, 1935.

BLIGH, John, S.J.: *Ordination to the Priesthood*, London and New York, Sheed and Ward, 1956.

Butler's Lives of the Saints (edited, revised and supplemented by Herbert Thurston, S.J. and Donald Attwater), four volumes, London, Burns and Oates, and New York, Kenedy, 1956.

CONNELLY, J.: *Hymns of the Roman Liturgy*, London and New York, Longmans, 1954.

DUCHESNE, L.: *Christian Worship, its Origin and Evolution*, London, S.P.C.K., 1903.

EISENHOFER, Ludwig, and LECHNER, Joseph: *The Liturgy of the Roman Rite*, Edinburgh and New York, Nelson, 1961.

FELTOE, C. L.: *Sacramentarium leonianum*, Cambridge and New York, Cambridge Univ. Press, 1906.

GREENWELL, W. (Editor): *Egbert's Pontifical*, Surtees Society, 1854.

HAMMAN, A., O.F.M. (Editor): *Early Christian Prayers*, translated by Walter Mitchell, London, Longmans, and Chicago, Regnery, 1961.

HOFINGER, Johannes, S.J. (Editor): *Liturgy and the Missions: the Nijmegen Papers*, London, Burns and Oates, and New York, Kenedy, 1960.

JUNGMANN, Josef A., S.J.: *The Early Liturgy, to the Time of Gregory the Great,* translated by Francis A. Brunner, C.SS.R., London, Darton, Longman and Todd, 1960, and Notre Dame, Ind., Univ. of Notre Dame Press, 1959; *The Mass of the Roman Rite, its Origins and Development* (Missarum Solemnia), translated by Francis A. Brunner, C.SS.R., two volumes, New York, Benziger, 1951 and 1956.

KLAUSER, Theodor: *The Western Liturgy and its History,* translated by F. L. Cross, London, Mowbray and New York, Morehouse-Gorham, 1952.

O'CONNELL, J. B.: *Sacred Music and Liturgy* (the Instruction of the S. Congregation of Rites translated with a Commentary), London, Burns and Oates, 1959.

PUNIET, P. de, O.S.B.: *The Roman Pontifical, A History and Commentary,* London and New York, Longmans, 1932.

SHEPPARD, Lancelot C.: *How to Use the New Breviary,* London, Darton, Longman and Todd, 1961.

SYMONS, T., O.S.B. (Editor): *Regularis Concordia,* Edinburgh and New York, Nelson, 1953.

VAN DIJK, S. J. P., O.F.M. and WALKER, J. Hazelden: *The Origins of the Modern Roman Liturgy,* London, Darton, Longman and Todd, and Westminster, Md, Newman Press, 1960.

WILSON, H. A.: *The Gelasian Sacramentary,* London and New York, Oxford Univ. Press, 1894; *The Gregorian Sacramentary,* London, Henry Bradshaw Society, 1915.